Secrets of the Second Mile

How to Overcome Life's Obstacles and Live in Victory

MARK CROW

SECRETS OF THE SECOND MILE: HOW TO OVERCOME LIFE'S OBSTACLES AND LIVE IN VICTORY
ISBN: 1-933188-03-0
Copyright © 2005 by Mark Crow
Printed in the United States of America
All rights reserved.
Second printing January, 2006

Published by:
  HonorNet
  P.O. Box 910
  Sapulpa, OK 74067

Dedication

This book is dedicated to Nadine and Harold Crow,

my mom and dad, who taught me to go the second

mile, no matter the cost. Thanks for living a "second-

mile life," for always doing more than you were

asked to do, and for challenging me to do the same.

*You are **awesome parents** and wonderful people.*

*The two hardest things in life are
starting and finishing.*

Foreword

Most people just drift along in life, never really beginning, creating, or trying anything new. Because they don't start anything, they never have to worry about finishing anything—life is easy, if not a little boring. Then there are a smaller number of people who enjoy starting things. They love to get new things going. But that's all they do. They start things but never manage to finish what they've begun. They may even start things with absolutely no interest or intention of ever finishing them.

Then, there are the history makers.

These are the people from that small group who actually finish what they start. They stick to the task, no matter what, and complete the job that God gives them to do. This is why I understand Mark Crow so well—because he has made the unique decision to do whatever it takes to complete the task that God has given him. And that kind of decision, like taking the road less traveled, has made all the difference.

That's what this book is about.

With this book, Mark provides an inspiring work for anyone who is looking to make an impact on this world. *Secrets of the Second Mile* is full of "whatever-it-takes" ideas for "whatever-it-takes" type of people. In this book, you'll discover that traveling the second mile is about longevity, perseverance, dedication, and sacrifice. It's about not getting sidetracked the minute any distraction crosses your path or giving up if your God-given mission doesn't "feel right." It's about sticking to it until you finish the race. It's about staying in one place, if necessary, and doing the same thing for months, years, even decades—if that's what it takes.

Because it's how you finish that counts.

On the night Jesus was betrayed, He brought His disciples to a quiet garden, and there He gave them instructions. He told them to keep going because He knew what was coming.

He knew the end was near.

But the disciples were tired, and they gradually began to sink to the ground. Jesus had asked them to keep praying—to keep focused on the difficult hours ahead so that they would be able to finish the race they had begun with the Savior. But that's not what they did.

One by one, they slumped over on the ground—and slept. Only Jesus kept going.

While the others finished their ministry with Jesus by sleeping, Jesus finished His ministry by going farther into the garden, staying there a little longer, and praying a little harder. And there, alone, away from all the others, He committed Himself to the cross. This is how Jesus gave up His life—for you, for me. By going farther, staying longer, and praying harder.

Jesus went the second mile.

That's one of the reasons I like Jesus. He's a second-mile Person, and I like second-mile people. You don't meet them very often, probably because they're rare these days. But you can look back through history and find many of them. Just think of David Livingstone, who gave his life for Africa upon hearing one simple phrase describing "the smoke of a thousand villages where no missionary had ever been."[1] History remembers second-mile people because second-mile people make history. These are the ones who change the course of the world by their persistence and their faith.

How do you spot a second-mile person? It's easy.

You just look for the "thousand-yard stare." You've seen it. It's the look these people get when they've been through too many battles for too many years. All the memories stay with them, and at times they get lost and stare into the distance as the thoughts of all the disappointments, the betrayals, the sacrifices, and the scars flash through their mind. You have to walk a long road to earn that "thousand-yard stare," but don't fool yourself: You must earn it. Just ask any war veteran, emergency-room doctor, recovering drug addict, or New York City firefighter.

Just ask Mark Crow.

Mark Crow understands what it
takes to go the second mile.

When I look at Mark, I see that "thousand-yard stare." I saw it when we met over fifteen years ago. Even at that time, he had already come through so much. But I knew all those years ago that Mark had an enormous dream for an enormous ministry. But sometimes you have to fight pretty hard to see your dreams come true. I have seen in Mark everything it takes to build a mega-ministry with worldwide impact. I see a person who is willing to go the second mile.

That's what it takes to build the kind of ministry that will change the world. A life that is willing. Mark Crow understands something that I've been saying for years, but that so few people truly understand: *It doesn't matter if you stumble along the way, get beat up, struggle, lose all of your money, get sick, or suffer persecution* (all things I know Mark Crow has gone through in his life and ministry), *it's only where you finish that matters.* This is why I'm so confident that no other person is more qualified to write this book than Mark Crow.

Mark understands from his incredible experience that if you go the second mile, or the third, or the fourth—if you just keep going—you can impact individuals, cities, and even nations for eternity.

So when it comes time for you to enter your own garden, and that time *will* come someday, take this book with you. Take it with you for the second mile . . . and for the third mile and the fourth and on and on.

When that time comes, remember to go a little farther, stay a little longer, and pray a little harder. World changers always finish strong.

Bill Wilson
Founder and Director,
Metro Ministries
Brooklyn, New York
October 11, 2002

Contents

*The Bible describes the
Christian life as a race that is
to be run with determination
and completed in victory.*

Introduction

The race to which we have been called is nothing like a sprint or a 100-yard dash. This race will take a lifetime to complete. Although we often endure conflict and hardship as we run, our race was never designed to defeat us. Rather, it is the place that has been designed for us in which we will receive God's richest blessings as we emerge victorious.

Just as an athlete begins a race filled with enthusiasm and determination, we begin our Christian life with the joyous expectation of a victorious life in

Christ. We jump off the starting line full of energy. However, after the thrill of the first mile begins to wear off, we often find ourselves facing difficulties and challenges as we begin the second mile.

Too often new believers are led to think that a life devoted to the Lord promises blessings and a guarantee that all of their problems will be minimized or even eliminated. The truth is, difficult situations come to us whether we are living for God or not: *"He causes his sun to rise on the evil and the good, and sends rain on the righteous and the unrighteous"* (Matthew 5:45). But as Christians, there is a way to handle life's difficulties that will assure our victory in the end.

The writer of Hebrews has this to say:

Therefore, since we are surrounded by such a great cloud of witnesses, let us throw off everything that hinders and the sin that so easily entangles, and let us run with perseverance the race marked out for us. Let us fix our eyes on Jesus, the author and perfecter of our faith, who for the joy set before him endured the cross, scorning its shame, and sat down at the right hand of the throne of God.

—Hebrews 12:1–2

Jesus understood that victory only comes when you stay in the race long enough to cross the finish line. Just as an athlete prepares and trains for the trials that he will face in a race, we, too, can learn the secrets of running the race of life in such a way as to finish victorious.

As I have run my own race of life, I have learned a number of principles that have helped me to continue on toward a strong and victorious completion of the purpose God has for my life. It is my prayer that as you read this book, these principles will help you to run with endurance the second mile in your life. Pay attention to what God has to say to you as you read these words. Take note of the "mile markers" along the way—questions designed to help you think through the principles that are presented and apply them to your own life. With proper training and instruction, diligence and perseverance on your part, and the help and strength of the Holy Spirit, you are destined to finish in victory!

Victory belongs to the most persevering.
—Napoleon I

*Victory at all costs, victory in spite of all terror,
victory however long and hard the road may
be; for without victory, there is no survival.*
—Winston Churchill

Run in such a way as to get the prize.
—1 Corinthians 9:24

On Your Mark, Get Set, Go!

Sally Robbins was a member of Australia's 2004 Olympic rowing team, competing in the women's eight final. Unfortunately, with approximately 400 meters left in the race, the twenty-three-year-old athlete suddenly quit. As Robbins slumped and let her oar dip into the water, Australia dropped from third to last place in the event.

"I just rowed my guts out in the first 1,500 and didn't have anything left. That's all I could have done for today," Robbins explained.

Her teammates were not sympathetic, even threatening to throw her into the water. In a country that takes its rowing extremely seriously, the *Sydney Daily Telegraph*'s headline read: "Just Oarful." It went on to ask readers to vote on whether or not Robbins had cost her team a medal. Melbourne's newspaper headline read: "It's eight, mate, pull your weight," underscoring the fact that Robbins' actions had hurt her entire team.

Even so, Robbins is optimistic about her chances of someday returning to competition with her teammates, despite their setback in the Olympics: "It'll be a long process, and I think that I will be back, and will be back with these girls, again, eventually," she said. "Obviously, I have to earn back their trust." Whether that feeling will ever be shared by her teammates remains to be seen.[1]

Unfortunately, Sally Robbins realized shortly into her race that the "second mile" is not as easy as most of us think it is. My own story also demonstrates how a race—both physical and spiritual—can get much tougher after the first mile.

In 1990, the Holy Spirit impressed upon me to do something that would call attention to the needs of young, unmarried pregnant women and their unborn children. So I decided to run a long-distance marathon of my own making from Tulsa, Oklahoma, to Washington, D.C.

On the first mile of that journey, I was so energized that I could have eaten an apple with one hand and juggled with the other. But then came the second mile. Followed by many, many more. During the weeks I spent on the road during that time, the Holy Spirit began to teach me about the secrets of the second mile. As each mile on my journey passed, the run got a little tougher. But it was the last miles of my race that pulled out of me the strength and perseverance it took to bring a victorious end to the race God had given me to run.

Just four years after that run across America, my wife, Jennifer, and I left the security of our home and jobs at a church in Victoria, Texas, and moved our family to Oklahoma City, where we knew only two other people! When we arrived, all we had were our four children, our belongings, and a vision to reach a city, change a nation, and touch the world with the Gospel of Jesus Christ.

The lessons I had learned on my run across America, the secrets of the second mile, I began to apply to every aspect of the new work God had set before me. Since our start in Oklahoma City, we have seen God's vision unfold in more spectacular ways than we could ever have imagined. Victory Christian Center, in Oklahoma City, was founded in August 1994, and in the last ten years, has grown to an active church family numbering over 8,000. In addition to the establishment of two schools within the church, we have begun numerous local outreaches into our community and state, and we are involved in mission work on virtually every continent around the globe. Our services are aired on local and regional television stations in the United States, as well as in twenty-two other nations throughout Europe. And we are watched live by thousands worldwide on the Internet. Together, we are proclaiming God's message of the victorious life He provides for us in Jesus Christ to our city, our state, our nation, and the world.

Now, you may be thinking, *Well, all that second-mile stuff is fine for you, Pastor, because you are in ministry, and you have built a church from the ground up.* I haven't told you my story in order to brag about the things we have done or to congratulate myself in any way. I share these things with you to give all the glory to God and to acknowledge what He is willing to do with someone who is willing to go the second mile. If you are a Christian, I can assure you that God has a plan and a purpose for your life, including a race that He intends for you to run—and to win. It may not be a physical run across the nation, or a bid for an Olympic medal in rowing, but it is a race nonethe- less—a race to fulfill the purpose and destiny to which He has called you and designed your life. The good news is that He has already equipped you to do it!

> *Everyone born of God overcomes the world. This is the victory that has overcome the world, even our faith. Who is it that overcomes the world? Only he who believes that Jesus is the Son of God.*
> —1 John 5:4–5

In the race that is set out before you, there will be long stretches of highway that will test your endurance. They are part of the course of every Christian's life. But

Christians have been given a road map that tells us how to both train for and run the race in such a way as to ensure victory—God's Word. The Scriptures are filled with promises of victory to those who follow its instruction.

> *The LORD your God is the one who goes with you to fight for you against your enemies to give you victory.*
> —Deuteronomy 20:4

> *Thanks be to God! He gives us the victory through our Lord Jesus Christ.*
> —1 Corinthians 15:57

> *I have fought a good fight, I have finished the race, and I have remained faithful. And now the prize awaits me—the crown of righteousness that the Lord, the righteous Judge, will give me on that great day of his return.*
> —2 Timothy 4:7–8 NLT

However, in light of these scripture passages that promise victory when we persevere through our circumstances, Jesus' words to His disciples in Matthew 5:38–42 seem rather incongruous:

"You have heard that it was said, 'Eye for eye, and tooth for tooth.' But I tell you, Do not resist an evil person. If someone strikes you on the right cheek, turn to him the other also. And if someone wants to sue you and take your tunic, let him have your cloak as well. If someone forces you to go one mile, go with him two miles. Give to the one who asks you, and do not turn away from the one who wants to borrow from you."

This passage of scripture has always intrigued me, especially what Jesus said in verse 41: *"If someone forces you to go one mile, go with him two miles."* Because I am a runner, I was particularly drawn to this statement. As I read this verse over and over and meditated on its meaning, I wondered, *What, exactly, did Jesus mean when He said to go the second mile? Why does God want us to do such a thing? What happens on the second mile that might have the potential to change my life?*

Jesus' meaning in the context of this passage is clear: As Christians, we are required to do more than what is asked of us in any given situation. We are not only to tolerate our enemies, but we are to extend to them the hand of kindness, friendship, and love. We are not called to just pay our tithes; we are called to give offerings to the Lord out of an overflow of love in our hearts for Him. We are not to expect the mediocre; we are to believe for the impossible! God asks that we go beyond our comfort zones, do more than is asked, go the second mile. The reality is that there are spiritual principles that are tied to our growth and victory that are only activated if we are willing to endure and "do what it takes."

To fully understand Jesus' statement in this passage, we must first understand the context in which it was spoken—the times in which Jesus and His disciples were living. They lived under the harsh oppression of Roman rule. The tax revenues that were generated within the Roman Empire itself did not cover all of the army's expenses, and therefore, Roman soldiers could demand, as a legal right they had been given, that Jewish inhabitants of their empire provide them with forced labor at their command. The law mandated that if a Roman soldier invoked this legal right by asking a Jewish subject to carry his armor or assist him with any other personal possessions, that person would be required to do so for one mile, but no more, although many soldiers abused this right and would stretch the distance or use multiple laborers in order to move their goods and possessions.

What benefits did Jesus possibly think could be gained from submitting to what most people at that time would perceive to be unjust demands of the occupying forces? The words of Jesus strike at the very core of human sensibilities—and selfishness: *"If someone forces you to go one mile, go with him two miles"* (Matthew 5:41).

Jesus was advocating not only *compliance*, that is, merely doing what was asked, but *active cooperation* with a member of the occupying army—in other words, the enemy. Jesus was clearly asking His followers—both then and today—to value others above themselves and to even go beyond what the law required.

Going the extra mile involves not only submitting to unjust demands but actually *exceeding* them. Why does our Lord make such a request of us? What could possibly be accomplished in the spiritual life of the believer when this mandate is met?

It would be reasonable to speculate that the religious Scribes and Pharisees would have submitted to the letter

of the law and would have carried the soldiers' possessions for one mile. The law would have been obeyed—
but that would certainly have been all they would have
done! Jesus is clearly much more interested in what
takes place within our spirits when we willingly submit
to Him and choose to gladly and cheerfully go beyond
what is required. Jesus knew that there are spiritual
principles that can only be learned, released, and
applied in our lives when we choose to take the road less
traveled: These are the secrets of the second mile.

Two roads diverged in a wood, and I—
I took the one less traveled by,
And that has made all the difference.
                                        —Robert Frost

Let's begin this journey together as we turn to the
first secret: *The second mile is a place of miracles.*

MILE MARKERS

- *"If someone forces you to go one mile, go with him two miles"* (Matthew 5:41). What does this statement of Jesus mean to you?

- Going the second mile is often seen as the unpopular choice, even the "road less traveled." How might taking this unpopular route "make all the difference" and change your life?

- In what ways have you gone the second mile recently? In what ways is God calling you to go further, perhaps even beyond the second mile?

We conquer by continuing.
—George Matheson

Be strong! It matters not how
deep entrenched the wrong
How hard the battle goes,
the day how long
Faint not—fight on!
tomorrow comes the song.
—Malthie D. Babcock

Let us not become weary in doing
good, for at the proper time we will
reap a harvest if we do not give up.
Therefore, as we have opportunity,
let us do good to all people.
—Galatians 6:9–10

A Place of Miracles

Steven Bradbury of Australia hasn't always been known for his prowess on the ice. In fact, you might say he is an accident just waiting for a televised event to happen.

In 1994, Bradbury cut his leg in a World Cup skating competition and almost bled to death, losing four liters of blood and receiving 111 stitches. In 2000, he crashed headfirst into the board while training and broke his neck. Although his doctors told him that if he ever skated again, he would risk permanent paralysis, he defied the odds and staged a comeback in time for the 2002 Winter Olympic games in Salt Lake City.

Steven Bradbury was, in many commentators' opinions, the least likely skater to win a medal—any medal—at the games. And yet he took home the gold.

Bradbury's victory is remarkable not only because he had encountered many setbacks and defeats, but because he won the gold medal after the other four skaters in the event *fell down* just before the finish. You could almost see Bradbury thinking, *I'm still standing up. I'm crossing the finish line. I just won the race!* In a split second, he had skated from last place to first—but only because he hadn't quit.[1]

The second mile is a place of miracles.

What about you? Like Steven Bradbury, do you feel like you should be voted "least likely to win" in the circumstances of your life? If so, take heart! Jesus Himself has called us to walk the second mile with Him—to press on and persevere, to do something unexpected to gain the victory—and when we are obedient, we will see miracles take place in our lives.

We have all experienced times in our lives when we have done everything we could possibly do in an impossible situation, yet the only result seemed to be mental and emotional exhaustion. But as Chuck Swindoll once said, "We are all faced with innumerable opportunities brilliantly disguised as impossible situations."[2] Such circumstances should indicate to us that we have embarked on the second mile of our race . . . and the second mile is a place of miracles!

Before our path can intersect with our second-mile miracle, however, we will always experience the demand that God puts on our faith. I'm not talking about the kind of demand that adds "one more thing" to an already heavy load that we carry, but rather, the kind of demand it takes to pull a treasure out of a hidden reservoir. The reason we experience this pull on our faith is so that, in this place Jesus calls the second mile, we can find the miracle that God has prepared for us.

One woman whom Jesus encountered experienced this "pull" on her faith before she received her miracle:

A large crowd followed and pressed around him [Jesus]. And a woman was there who had been subject to bleeding for twelve years. She had suffered a great deal under the care of many doctors and had spent all she had, yet instead of getting better she grew worse. When she heard about Jesus, she came up behind him in the crowd and touched his cloak, because she thought, "If I just touch his clothes, I will be healed." Immediately her bleeding stopped and she felt in her body that she was freed from her suffering.

—Mark 5:24–29

This is a rather graphic description of a woman who had done everything she was able to do, yet nothing in her situation changed. Can you relate? She could have given up, but instead she chose to press through the crowd to get to Jesus. And when Jesus saw her perseverance, her persistence to press through and go the second mile to attain her healing, He said to her,

"Daughter, your faith has healed you. Go in peace and be freed from your suffering" (Mark 5:34). The pull on her faith caused her to connect with the miracle that she so needed in her life.

Maria Lopez experienced this pull on her faith—but she held to what she knew to be true, and eventually discovered that the second mile brought her the miracle she so desperately needed.

Every other Tuesday, Maria would come to clean Barbara's house. She always arrived like a bubble of energy, determined to restore order to Barbara's universe, scrubbing as though it were an act of worship.

As the two became acquainted, Barbara learned that Maria was a pastor's daughter from Peru who had no family in the United States. Barbara had only been a Christian for a few years, and she grew to appreciate Maria's enthusiastic faith. She prayed out loud while she cleaned, and she sang praise songs in Spanish while she scrubbed. She praised Jesus everywhere she went.

One Tuesday, Maria didn't show up for work. Barbara anticipated seeing her cheery face the following day, but no one came. When she didn't arrive on the third day, Barbara called her house, but no one answered the phone.

This is so unlike her, Barbara thought. *She's usually so reliable. There must be a good reason.*

Three days later, a nurse called to say that Maria was in the hospital. Alarmed, Barbara cut some flowers and drove to the hospital to find out what was wrong. When she arrived, she found Maria sitting up in bed, rocking back and forth with her head encased in a heavy iron cage resting on her shoulders. Her eyes were closed, and tears streamed down her cheeks. Barbara touched her arm gently and held out the flowers. She clutched them to her chest.

"What's that around your head, Maria?"

"Oooh, Meessus," she moaned, touching the iron contraption, "it is the torture of Satan."

Puzzled, Barbara turned to the nurse, who explained: "It's called a halo. It's screwed and bolted directly into the skull in four different places. It isn't pleasant."

"How long do you have to wear it?" Barbara asked Maria.

"Five months, my doctor say, maybe. But Meessus, you tell him, Maria, she no live five months with thees in her head. She die. You tell him, yes?"

"I'll talk to him, Maria. Anything else I can do for you?"

"Yes, Meessus. My Bible." She pointed to the bedside table. "Please, you read to me." Barbara started reading John 14: *"Do not let your hearts be troubled. Trust in God; trust also in me."*

Out in the corridor, Barbara found Maria's doctor. "Why is she wearing that hideous device?" she asked.

"Because, to put it simply, if she didn't," he said, "her head would literally fall off. Maria has cancer. Her neck bones have degenerated to the point where they can no longer support her head."

"Can they be repaired? Or regenerated?"

The doctor shook his head gravely. "It means we can't ever take the halo off. Maria will have to learn to live with it."

Every week when Barbara visited, Maria asked her to pray with her and read from the Bible. She always requested the same chapter from the New Testament: John 14. Weeks turned into months. The heavy metal halo was crippling.

During one visit, months after being admitted to the hospital, Maria clutched Barbara's hands and whispered,

"God tells Maria it won't be long. Soon, He say, we take this off."

Before Barbara left the hospital, she stopped at the nurses' desk to ask how much longer Maria would be there. A nurse informed her that they were preparing papers to release Maria. "Unfortunately, Maria doesn't have enough insurance money left to stay in the hospital, so they're sending her home."

Maria panicked when the doctor told her she would be going home. "No! You take new x-ray!" Touching the halo, she cried, "You take this torture from me! I no leave with this!"

"There really is no point in another x-ray," the doctor insisted. "Nothing has changed."

When Barbara returned to the hospital two days later to pick up Maria, she was surprised to find her sitting in a chair, beaming from ear to ear. "I no leave today," she said.

"Why not, Maria? Have you had your x-ray?"

"Yes. But I stay until they take this off." She rolled her eyes toward the halo.

Hasn't anyone told Maria what will happen when they take the halo off? It was Barbara's turn to panic. *I can't tell her. Her despair will be overwhelming.*

Barbara cornered the doctor in the hall. "She won't leave until you take the halo off. What should we do?"

"We'll take it off," he replied.

"You said her head would roll off without it!"

Suddenly Maria's doctor began acting strangely. He looked left and right, then began to mutter in low tones. "It won't roll. The x-ray we took this morning indicated that her neck bones have regenerated."

"You said that was impossible!"

"It is impossible."

Barbara shook her head, confused. "Were the original x-rays a mistake?"

"Not at all. They're here for anyone to see."

"So?"

Before answering, the doctor sighed. "So . . . there are things I can't explain. Her bones have regenerated, and they are strong enough to hold her head. That's all I know."

"Doctor! Is this a miracle?"

"I don't know about miracles," the doctor answered. "That's Maria's department. She tells me that Jesus healed her."[3]

Like the woman with the issue of blood, Maria had suffered much in her medical treatments, and it took a financial toll on her resources. But also like the woman in the Bible, Maria had faith that her persistence would bring her a miracle. She pressed on through the second mile to "touch the hem of Jesus' garment," and just as He did 2,000 years ago, He moved in her life with compassion and power. The second mile is a place of miracles!

So often, even when we are exercising our faith, we may be tempted to stop when we are tired and there is nothing else we know to do in a situation. But hear me on this: We may run out of energy, but we must never run out of faith! That is the point when God begins pulling on our faith, because He knows that we are capable of pressing through to the second mile.

A group of four men in the New Testament were determined to help their paralyzed friend go the second mile and reach the place of healing:

So many gathered that there was no room left, not even outside the door, and he [Jesus] preached the word to them. Some people came, bringing to him a paralytic, carried by four of them. Since they could not get him to Jesus because of the crowd, they made an opening in the roof above Jesus and, after digging through it, lowered the mat the paralyzed man was lying on. He said to the paralytic, "I tell you, get up, take your mat and go home." He got up, took his mat and walked out in full view of them all.

—Mark 2:2–4, 10–12

These four men had already gone the first mile just to get their paralyzed friend to Jesus. They might have said, "We have inconvenienced ourselves. We are tired and sweaty. And now that we are here with such a great need, nobody is listening to us, and we can't even get in the door!" But instead of giving up, they responded to God's pull on their faith, went the second mile, and received the miracle they needed.

Sometimes we need to be the ones to help carry others the second mile when they can't do it for themselves. If you are believing God for His intervention in the life of someone you know, don't give up! Just as Jesus honored the faith of the friends of the paralytic,

He loves to honor our faith for others when we stand strong and press on through the second mile.

Lindsey O'Connor was unable to believe God for her own healing, but her friends and loved ones pressed on in her behalf. Lindsey was in the midst of a two-month coma, brought on by complications from childbirth. Her family was told to expect brain damage, and the doctors believed that her death was only a matter of time.

Her husband, Tim, faced the possibility of a brain-damaged wife, and caring singlehandedly for five children, including a newborn. Still, he refused to issue the "Do Not Resuscitate" order, believing instead for a miracle.

Lindsey herself describes this critical time:

I remember Tim holding one of my hands, a neurologist the other, and telling me to squeeze their hands. Unable to do so or to speak, I felt my brain screaming, "Why can't I do this? Maybe I'm dying." Later, my inability to use the call button left me banging a spoon on the bedside table for an hour and a half. No one came. They thought it was the repetitive motor response of a brain-damaged woman.

Two weeks after the initial dance on the edge came a death vigil. As I lay dying, the respirator whirred, pumping air into my lifeless-looking body and then sucking it out. . . . My limbs were blue and as cold as refrigerated meat. It did not look like I had any upper-level brain function. I was expected to die before morning.

I later learned that forty or more friends and relatives stood vigil in the waiting room, praying for my recovery.

The prayers of Lindsey's friends and relatives were able to carry her the second mile, to the place of miracles. One day, not long after her brush with death, Lindsey woke up. It was weeks before she could speak, but she was going to live.

I went into the hospital on August 30, 2002, and came home just before Christmas, still unable to walk or breathe on my own. In spite of daily physical effects of the trauma, I've learned that radical obedience (in my case, having a baby at forty) is worth any cost, that prayer is inconceivably important, that miracles still happen, and that I have a faith worth dying for.[4]

Although both Maria and Lindsey had a support system in their struggle to carry on through the second mile, not everyone is so fortunate. The Bible tells of two blind men whose second mile included persistence in the face of opposition from others.

Two blind men were sitting by the roadside, and when they heard that Jesus was going by, they shouted, "Lord, Son of David, have mercy on us!"

The crowd rebuked them and told them to be quiet, but they shouted all the louder, "Lord, Son of David, have mercy on us!"

Jesus stopped and called them, "What do you want me to do for you?" he asked.

"Lord," they answered, "we want our sight."

Jesus had compassion on them and touched their eyes. Immediately they received their sight and followed him.

—Matthew 20:30–34

I can only imagine what the first mile was like for these two men. They could have accepted their blindness and just stayed home, but instead they found a place on the road where Jesus would be traveling. That is where they experienced the pull on their faith that put them in the place of miracles.

The Scriptures tell us that the crowd rebuked the blind men and told them to be quiet. Many of us, when we experience a rebuke, simply withdraw and say to ourselves, *I have been rebuked and wounded, and I just don't know what I am going to do.* The thing to do is to take a lesson from the blind guys who simply shouted all the louder!

There is a shift in the story when Jesus stopped and called to the blind men. Those who had been responsible for rebuking the men were probably thinking, *See—we told them to shut up, and they didn't. Now Jesus is really going to give it to them!* Imagine their shock as Jesus responded to their faith by healing them.

Those two blind men made the decision that they were not going to continue living the way they had been living and experiencing what they had been experiencing. They were determined to get the miracle they needed from Jesus, and they were willing to go the second mile to get it.

Have you experienced persecution for your persistence in your faith? Consider the story of Hawa Ahmed. Hawa was a Muslim student in North Africa. One day, she read a Christian tract in her dormitory and decided to become a Christian. Her father was a ruler in the Islamic faith, and so she expected to lose her inheritance because of her conversion. She was completely unprepared for what actually took place.

When Hawa told her family that she had become a Christian and had changed her name to Faith, her father exploded in rage. Her father and brothers stripped her naked and bound her to a chair fixed to a metal plate with which they planned to electrocute her. Faith asked them to at least lay a Bible in her lap. Her father responded, "If you want to die together with your false religion, so be it." One of her brothers added, "That will show that your religion is powerless."

Although they had bound her, Faith was able to touch a corner of the Bible. She felt a strange peace, as though someone were standing beside her. Her father and brothers pushed the plug into the socket—and nothing happened. They tried four times with various cables, but it was as though the electricity refused to flow. Finally her father, frustrated and angry, hit her and screamed, "You are no longer my daughter!"

Faith's family threw her into the street, naked. But as she ran through the city streets, humiliated and in pain, people began to look at her curiously, rather than in shock. Shaking and tearful, she ran to a friend's house. Her friend let her in, clothed her, and gave her shelter. The next day, her friend asked neighbors what they had thought when they had seen Faith running naked through the streets. "What are you talking about?" they asked. "The girl had on a beautiful white dress. We were asking ourselves why someone so beautifully clothed had to run through the streets." God had hidden her nakedness from their eyes, clothing her in a beautiful white dress.

Faith ran the second mile, persevering in her faith even though she knew it would cost her dearly. And she reached the place of miracles. Today, Faith is a full-time evangelist with Every Home for Christ, helping to spread the message of God's love around the world.

Perhaps the persecution you face in your life is not to the degree that Faith experienced. Maybe you don't face rebukes and opposition as the blind men did in Jesus' day. But make no mistake, the second mile is not always an easy journey to take. It will require a pull on your faith that you may never have experienced before, but it always results in miracles taking place in your life.

The faith to go the second mile
already lies within you.

You may have already done everything possible in an impossible situation, and are at the place where you are mentally and emotionally exhausted. You may feel as if you just can't take any more because you are worn out. But I want to encourage you that the faith to go the second mile already lies within you. All you have to do is respond to God's pull on that faith, and you will find that you don't have to give up, give out, or give in. You will find that the second mile will be your place of miracles.

MILE MARKERS

- Have you ever had to be persistent in your faith before you received a miracle? What was the situation? What was the result?

- Has there ever been a time in your life when your friends or loved ones carried you through the second mile to the place of miracles? Have you ever carried another person on this journey of faith?

- When have you experienced opposition to your faith? What was your reaction? How did this opposition strengthen—or weaken—your faith?

- In your own life, how have you seen the second mile as a "place of miracles"?

*Preach the gospel of Jesus Christ wherever
you go. If necessary, use words.*
—Saint Francis of Assisi

*The most important single influence in the
life of a person is another person . . .
who is worthy of emulation.*
—Paul D. Shafer

Example moves the world more than doctrine.
—Henry Miller

*Dear brothers and sisters, pattern
your lives after mine, and learn from
those who follow our example.*
—Philippians 3:17 NLT

Setting an Example for Others

3

Did you know that the size of the rocket boosters in our modern-day space program was actually determined by ancient Roman chariots? Boyd Clarke and Ron Crossland explain:

The U.S. standard railroad gauge is four feet, eight-and-a-half inches. How did we wind up with such an odd railway width? Because that was the width English railroad-building expatriates brought with them to America. Why did the English build them this wide? Because the first British rail lines were built by the same people who built the pre-railroad tramways, and that's the gauge they used. Why did they use that gauge? Because the same jigs, tools, and people who built wagons built the tramways and used the standard wagon-wheel spacing. Wagon-wheel spacing was standardized due to a very practical, hard-to-change, and easy-to-match reality. When Britain was ruled by Imperial Rome, Roman war chariots, in true bureaucratic fashion, all used standard spacing between their wheels.

Over time, this spacing left deep ruts along the extensive road network the Romans built. If British wheel spacing didn't match Roman ruts, the wheels would break. The Roman standard was derived after trial-and-error efforts of early wagon and chariot builders. They determined the best width that would accommodate two horse butts was four feet, eight-and-a-half inches. Thus the United States' standard railroad gauge is a hand-me-down standard based upon the original specification for an Imperial Roman war chariot.

This doesn't end at railroads. Two big booster rockets attach to the sides of the main fuel tank that lifts the space shuttle into orbit. Thiokol makes these solid-rocket boosters, SRBs, at its Utah factory. The engineers who design the SRBs ship them from factory to launch site by train. The railroad from the factory runs through a mountain tunnel only slightly wider than the railroad track. Even if Thiokol engineers wanted fatter SRBs, the railway gauge limits their design. Modern space-shuttle design follows horses' butts![1]

It's hard to imagine that the size of the modern booster rockets for our space shuttles today is based on something as "primitive" (in our minds, at least) as the length chosen for an ancient Roman chariot. But beyond that, I wonder what the designer of the chariot, who lived thousands of years ago, would think if he knew how far his estimation of "four horse-butt lengths" would travel! Sometimes you never know just how extensive your sphere of influence will be!

The second mile is a place where
we set an example for others.

When we travel the second mile, we enter a place where we can set the best example for others—because the greatest victories are always won by those who are willing to go just a little farther. Winners are those who have their priorities in order, and they press on to allow their influence to reach as many other people as they can reach.

Renowned dogsled racer DeeDee Jonrowe has this to say about priorities—and about being an example for others:

I believe God has a purpose for my being a musher. If I'm noted for something, I want it to be that I took good care of my dogs, kept the faith, and my integrity never wavered. There was a time when I got carried away with the sport and didn't give God or my husband their rightful places. It was about my ego. It was about winning. My reputation was tied up in my dogs. Finally, I came to understand God loves me whether I win or lose. That stands true, regardless how I feel.

DeeDee Jonrowe and her husband are active members of the Big Lake Baptist Church, where she teaches the children's story time. The congregation supports her racing by cooking and packaging her trail meals, answering fan mail, and recording music for her to enjoy while on the trail.

DeeDee doesn't carry a Bible with her on the Iditarod—exposure to the sun and snow make it impossible for her eyes to focus on small print. Church members type Bible verses on bookmark-sized cards and put them in the food parcels that are shipped to checkpoints. "They use a large font so I can read them," she says. "When I leave the checkpoint, the verses are left behind for others to read."

A week before the race, DeeDee and her husband, Mike, are called to the front during Sunday's worship service. The congregation forms a circle around them, and asks God for safety, for good judgment, and for God to help her do her best. After the Iditarod, the church always celebrates her safe return. They use it as an outreach, inviting the entire community to hear her speak.

Perhaps someday, DeeDee Jonrowe will add a first-place trophy to her bookshelf, but that's not her focus. She'd rather be an influence in the lives of other people. "I consider myself the caretaker of God's kennel," she says. "It's not about the place I finish in; it's about the integrity with which I do my job 365 days a year when no one's watching—or perhaps, if someone is watching. Do I still scoop and water? Do I pay attention to the quality of work, whether or not it means that I will win?"[2]

DeeDee Jonrowe has captured the concept of the second mile: that winning isn't always about finishing the race first—but it is always about setting a good example for others as you run!

I often enjoy reading what people who have a positive

influence on others have to say. One quote I particularly like is from Albert Schweitzer: "Example is not the main thing in influencing others; it is the *only* thing." Our greatest example in life should also be our greatest influence: Jesus Christ, who lived an exemplary life on earth and, through His death and resurrection, made it possible for us to follow in His footsteps.

On perhaps the most difficult night of His life, Jesus continued to set an example for us to follow even today as He prayed to His Father in the Garden of Gethsemane:

Then Jesus went with his disciples to a place called Gethsemane, and he said to them, "Sit here while I go over there and pray." He took Peter and the two sons of Zebedee along with him, and he began to be sorrowful and troubled. Then he said to them, "My soul is overwhelmed with sorrow to the point of death. Stay here and keep watch with me."

Going a little farther, he fell with his face to the ground and prayed, "My Father, if it is possible, may this cup be taken from me. Yet not as I will, but as you will."

He went away a second time and prayed . . .
and went away once more and prayed the third
time, saying the same thing.

—Matthew 26:36–39, 42, 44

What do you think was the greatest impression Jesus made that night? It was the fact that He went a little farther. Although He could have spent His time "whining" about having to go to the cross, He chose instead to accept God's will—and to pray.

The second mile is not something we are just called to run; we are called to run it without complaining, and we are called to run it in prayer. The second mile communicates our commitment to the cause, to the call, and to God's purpose for our lives.

How has Jesus been an example to you? How can you turn around and be an example of His love to others?

Joey Lee was in the race of his life—the 150-mile Marathon Des Sables, across the Moroccan Sahara Desert. On day four, Joey was still running, though other runners had already been airlifted out after surrendering to the heat or to physical exhaustion.

About 80 miles into the race, the air pockets in the soles of Joey's running shoes blew out, apparently from the heat. Joey was left with almost nothing to protect the soles of his feet as he ran over the sand and jagged rocks. Although he carried a backpack of provisions, it contained no extra shoes. His feet were blistered, his body exhausted from the 100-plus-degree temperatures. His eyes burned from the sand and sweat.

Facing another thirty miles to run that day, and forty more over the next three days, Joey refused to quit. The only sight ahead of him was the miles of desert, and the massive dunes he would have to overcome, but still he pressed on. Three days later, Joey finished the race in the middle of the pack of 600 other runners.

Joey Lee was running for a reason. His young wife, Allison, had died almost a year and a half earlier after a long battle with cancer. Joey was running in memory of his wife and to raise money for the American Cancer Society.

Ignoring the mental and physical obstacles he faced, he finished the race. Afterward, when asked what kept him going, he replied, "I just thought about

Allison a lot. This is nothing compared to what she went through."[3]

Joey Lee has been an inspiration to many people—as well as an example of what inspiration can do! He was inspired by his wife, and he, in turn, became an inspiration to others. The second mile is the place where we will set an example. As Jesus has been our example, we, in turn, can be an example to other people as we run our race with perseverance, giving all of the glory to God.

Perseverance is the key. Make your life an example of steadfastness—set your sights on the goal, and don't let anything sway you from continuing to run the race. The second mile commands, most of all, a commitment to the cause.

For example, good marriages begin in the first mile, but great marriages are built in the second mile. In his book *Sacred Marriage*, Gary Thomas notes that there are trees in Washington State's northern Cascades that are hundreds of years old. One tree in particular is 700 years old. Typically, forests experience damaging fires every fifty to sixty years. The reason the trees in the North Cascades live so long is because the drenching rains protect them from forest fires caused by lightning strikes. Gary Thomas comments:

> I think that's a good picture of a marriage that is based on the ministry of reconciliation. Strong Christian marriages will still be struck by lightning—sexual temptation, communication problems, frustrations, unrealized expectations—but if the marriages are heavily watered with an unwavering commitment to please God above everything else, the conditions won't be ripe for a devastating fire to follow the lightning strike.[4]

Gary Thomas notes that there were hundreds of trees in the forest, but the National Service put a sign in front of only one: the 700-year-old tree, because "it had survived seven centuries. It had simply gone the distance, and in so doing, it commanded attention."[5]

What an amazing statement of example! The tree

"commanded attention"—because it had "gone the distance"! That should be the picture of not just our marriages, but our entire lives.

The principles of the second mile don't just hold true in marriages; they can also have a lasting effect in families. It is in the second mile that the wayward family member finally comes home, because that is where we decide we will never stop behaving like believers and we will keep our faith in God.

An ancient Asian legend tells the story of a man who had a wild and impetuous son. Curtis E. Liens, in his book *The Man with Dirty Hands*, describes this legend:

The boy became involved with the ruffians of the village who persuaded him to join them in a robbery of his own father's treasury house. After the robbery was over, his friends fled with the stolen treasure and left him to face the guilt of the crime alone. The young man was desperate. He was deserted by his friends, and he had betrayed the trust of his father. But his greatest crime was that he had brought public dishonor on the family name. And in a culture where ancestors are worshiped and family integrity is a sacred trust, this was the worst wrong of all.

Broken and deeply repentant, he went to his father and begged forgiveness. Graciously, it was granted. The father called all of the members of the family together to celebrate the reconciliation and return of his son. When all had enjoyed the banquet to the fullest, the father stood and lifted his cup of rice wine for a toast. But as the son drank deeply the contents of his cup, he grabbed his throat and fell lifeless across the table. The son had been poisoned. The father, with ceremonial dignity, nodded to the guests. Each in turn graciously and politely bowed to the father as they silently left the banquet hall. All was now put right. The son had paid the price of his pardon with poison. His honor had been restored. The family integrity and honor were reestablished. The unfortunate incident was closed.[6]

What a sad story of what life without Christ is like! How tragic it would be if all of us had to pay for our sins ourselves! But what a striking contrast to Jesus' parable of the prodigal son, in which another father is deeply shamed by his son's wild and reckless behavior. But when that son comes back and begs forgiveness, what a different reaction he receives.

Jesus said, "There was a man who had two sons. The younger one said to his father, 'Father, give me my share of the estate.' So he divided his property between them.

"Not long after that, the younger son got together all he had, set off for a distant country and there squandered his wealth in wild living. After he had spent everything, there was a severe famine in that whole country, and he began to be in need. So he went and hired himself out to a citizen of that country, who sent him to his fields to feed pigs.

"When he came to his senses, he said, 'How many of my father's hired men have food to spare, and here I am starving to death! I will set out and go back to my father. . . .'

"But while he was still a long way off, his father saw him and was filled with compassion for him; he ran to his son, threw his arms around him and kissed him.

"The son said to him, 'Father, I have sinned against heaven and against you. I am no longer worthy to be called your son.'

"But the father said to his servants, 'Quick! Bring the best robe and put it on him. Put a ring on his finger and sandals on his feet. Bring the fattened calf and kill it. Let's have a feast and celebrate. For this son of mine was dead and is alive again; he was lost and is found.' So they began to celebrate."

—Luke 15:11–15, 17–18, 20–24

At the point at which the father bestowed the inheritance on his youngest son, both his legal and his moral obligations to his son were fulfilled. But I believe that before that young man ever left, his father made the decision to set an example by going farther than he was required to go. And he did it without complaining, just as Jesus did when He went to the cross on our behalf.

Although the entire community was probably buzzing with the news about the son's embarrassing new lifestyle, I can almost hear the father say, "I don't care what anybody else says about my son; someday he is going to come home." I can envision that father going to the tailor—who knew all about the family's problems—and asking him to make the finest robe for his son, with his initials on the outside and his name embroidered on the lining. Then I can see him hurrying to the cobbler and saying, "I want you to make the most superb pair of sandals for my son, who is coming home. You don't know it yet, and the tailor doesn't know it yet, but I know it on the inside because I am going the second mile."

Next he goes to the jeweler, whom the tailor has just informed about the young man's irresponsible behavior. The tailor proceeds to relate the information to the father and offers his opinion about the situation. But the father just looks at him and says, "I want you to make a ring, because my son is coming home!"

When we are on the second mile, it is important not to listen to the opinions of those who would tell us how things "ought to be." You see, the second mile is often filled with negativism, and although we cannot always avoid it, we can make the decision to go just a little farther.

When the son came home, he fully expected his father to make him a servant. Instead, the young man discovered that he had a second-mile daddy who welcomed him with love and forgiveness. This father's actions paint a picture of how our heavenly Father responds to us when we have made wrong decisions that pull us away from His plan for our lives.

When John Granger's son called, he was reluctant to answer. Through years of drug abuse, Scott had stolen from his family, manipulated his parents, and failed them over and over again. If John were to tell the truth, it had been a relief not to hear from Scott for two years.

But Scott told his father he'd been through a rehabilitation program a year and a half ago that had provided something no other had offered: a relationship with God. "I met Jesus Christ. I've been forgiven for my past. I want to ask you and Mom to forgive me, too." Scott said he was now helping other addicts get straightened out.

John was torn between hope and cynicism. The well-groomed, bright-eyed young man who arrived at the airport looked like a stranger. In the days that followed, Scott told how, in the midst of drug withdrawal, he'd seen a vision of Jesus Christ on the cross and cried out to Him for help. His withdrawal symptoms ended instantly. That experience had led him to a church. "I asked Jesus to be my Lord," he quietly explained, "and my life hasn't been the same since."[7]

The change in Scott was too dramatic for John and his wife to ignore. And soon, because of Scott's new amazing influence and his parents' second-mile mentality, Jesus gave them the same new life He had given their prodigal son.

Perhaps you are in a second-mile situation, even experiencing the criticism, negativism, and opinions of others. Consider the following very different perspectives that were taken on the day of the Normandy invasion in World War II.

On June 6, 1994, the fiftieth anniversary of the Allied invasion of Normandy took place. This invasion had begun the historic World War II battle to liberate continental Europe from Nazi control. All of the major television networks in the United States ran anniversary programs that included interviews with aging veterans.

One of the programs paired two contrasting interviews back to back. The first interview was conducted with a marine who had landed on Omaha Beach. He recalled horrors that sounded like scenes from Steven Spielberg's Academy Award-winning movie *Saving Private Ryan*. The aging veteran recalled looking around at the bloody casualties surrounding him and concluded, "We're going to lose!"

The next interview, however, was with a U.S. Army Air Corps reconnaissance pilot who had flown over the entire battle area. He viewed the carnage on the beaches and hills, but he also witnessed the successes of the marines, the penetration by the paratroopers, and the effectiveness of the aerial bombardment. He looked at everything that was happening and concluded, "We're going to win!"[8]

When you encounter the pessimism and negative attitudes that other people might have about your situation, always keep in mind that you have a higher Source to go to—and He says, "We're going to win!" But in order to achieve this victory, you must make up your mind that you are going to go a little farther, follow the example of Jesus, and be an example to others as you run the second mile.

The doctor told Marsha Mark and her husband that they needed to accept the fact that they would never have biological children. Amid the discouragement, Marsha clung to a friend's words: "Somehow, Marsha, God is going to use your struggle with infertility for His glory." Marsha began to pray for a glimpse of that glory. In her words:

I'd asked everyone I knew to pray. One five-year-old even gave God some suggestions: "Dear God, please send Marsha a baby. Maybe someone could give her one, or she could just find one on the street. Amen."

My husband stopped praying when we realized I was beginning menopause. Being a scientist, Tom had seen all the facts. And in his lifetime, he'd never seen prayer change facts.

Six months later, I made an appointment for some tests—including one more pregnancy test.

They looked at me with pity and said, "No. You haven't had any cycles for seven months. Asking for another pregnancy test indicates you are not accepting things as they are."

I begged for the extra test and finally convinced them. The test came back positive.

Over the next fourteen days, I had four more pregnancy tests and three more sonograms at the hospital's request. I think this time they were having trouble dealing with the facts.

My full-term pregnancy was uneventful—unless you count every day bathed in praise for the answer to our prayer. On October 22, 1996, Amanda Joy was born. We call her Miracle Mandy.[9]

Victory is within your reach! And when you achieve it, your life will begin to be an example to others of God's faithfulness to those who put their faith in Jesus Christ.

MILE MARKERS

➤ What role models have you had in your life who have inspired you to run the second mile?

➤ How can Jesus Himself be more of an example to you in the situations in which you currently find yourself?

➤ Who are the "doubters" and "naysayers" you are currently encountering? What does God have to say about your situation? How can you stay focused on His opinions and plans for your life?

➤ How can you be a positive example to others as you run the second mile?

I think and think for months, for years.
Ninety-nine times the conclusion is false.
The hundredth time I am right.
—Albert Einstein

Life, like war, is a series of mistakes, and he is best
who wins the most splendid victories by the
retrieval of mistakes.
—Frederick W. Robertson

Mishaps are like knives, that either serve us or cut
us, as we grasp them by the blade or the handle.
—James Russell Lowell

If we confess our sins to him, he is faithful and just
to forgive us and to cleanse us from every wrong.
—1 John 1:9 NLT

The Place of
Second Chances

In his quest to scale Mount Everest, Sir Edmund Hillary made several unsuccessful attempts before he finally succeeded. After one especially disheartening attempt, he stood at the base of the great mountain and shook his fist directly at it. "I'll defeat you yet!" he shouted in defiance. "Because you're as big as you're going to get—but I'm still growing!"[1]

Every time Sir Hillary climbed, he failed. And every time he failed, he learned. And every time he learned, he grew and tried again. And one day, he didn't fail.

The question has often been asked, "What great thing would you attempt—if you knew you couldn't fail?" Failure is part of the human experience, but you can make it work for you, if you refuse to give up—if you endure to enter the second mile.

The second mile is a place of second chances.

The second mile is where God gives us the opportunity to correct the mistakes that we made on the first mile! But if we don't press on to the second mile, we don't have the chance to fix the things we've done wrong. We don't get to see success spring from failure.

Some of the world's greatest success stories didn't always seem like such a success at the start. William Wrigley Jr., the founder of Wrigley Gum, ran away from home at the age of eleven to escape working in the family's soap manufacturing business. He went to New

York, where he sold newspapers, but soon was back home. In 1891 he left for good, going to Chicago to make his fortune. In the beginning, Wrigley continued to sell soap, offering a free can of baking powder as an incentive to his customers. Soap sales weren't strong, but people loved the baking powder, so he began to sell it exclusively, and added two pieces of gum as an incentive. He soon discovered that the gum was even more popular than the baking powder, so Wrigley then went into the gum business and made his fortune. Wrigley was actually a failure at selling soap—but through his failure, he found the way to his success![2]

Thankfully, Wrigley wasn't as great of a failure as Matt Emmons, favored to win the 2004 Olympic gold medal in the 50-meter three-position rifle event. It was in sight—he was one shot away from claiming victory. He didn't even need a bull's-eye to win. His final shot merely needed to be on the target.

Normally the shot he made would have received a score of 8.1, more than enough to win the gold. But in what was described as "an extremely rare mistake in elite competition," Emmons fired at the wrong target. Standing in lane two, he fired at the target in lane three. His score for a "good" shot at the "wrong" target?—0. Instead of a medal, Emmons ended up in eighth place.[3]

Matt's story would be comical, if it weren't so tragic. How many times do our failures occur because we are aiming at the wrong goal? It's time to focus on God, and determine what His goals for our lives are—and then go for it with everything we've got!

> *Our greatest fear should not be of failure, but of succeeding at something that doesn't really matter.*
> —Anonymous

One of my favorite second-mile characters who learned to overcome the failures in his life is Simon Peter, a man who actually had several notable accomplishments on the first mile of his journey. He had a revelation that Jesus was the Christ; he activated his faith and stepped out on the water to get to Jesus; and he was a witness to the Transfiguration. Peter was running a pretty good first mile—that is, until he cut off the ear of a Roman guard and then denied Jesus three times! Those are what we might call some major mistakes, but let's see what the Bible says about Peter as he emerged to begin his second mile.

> *Then they* [the apostles] *returned to Jerusalem from the hill called the Mount of Olives, a Sabbath day's walk from the city. When they arrived, they went upstairs to the room where they were staying. Those present were Peter, John, James and Andrew; Philip and Thomas, Bartholomew and Matthew; James son of Alphaeus and Simon the Zealot, and Judas son of James. They all joined together constantly in prayer, along with the women and Mary the mother of Jesus, and with his brothers.*
>
> *In those days Peter stood up among the believers (a group numbering about a hundred and twenty). . . .*
>
> —Acts 1:12–15

This group of 120 men and women were the first to be filled with the Holy Spirit, and the Scriptures say that Peter stood up among them. God knew that Peter had blown it, but like the prodigal father whom we discussed in the previous chapter, He already had things ready for Peter. Why? Because He is the God of a second chance. And because Peter was willing to go the second mile, thousands of people came to Jesus through his preaching, and many were miraculously healed and delivered.

Another familiar second-mile story is that of Jonah, who was told by God to go to Nineveh to preach the message of repentance. Jonah flat-out refused, and instead boarded a ship that was headed in another direction. He ended up getting thrown overboard in a storm, and was swallowed by a great fish. Talk about a first-mile mistake . . . Jonah's was a whopper!

When the fish vomited him out on dry land, God again said to Jonah, "Go to the great city of Nineveh and proclaim to it the message I give you" (Jonah 3:2). This time Jonah obeyed and went to the city for which the Lord had such great concern. It was in this second mile that Jonah got a second chance and the opportunity to correct the mistake he had made in the first mile.

You and I are no different than Peter and Jonah; we are going to make mistakes. But we have to be willing to go the second mile in order to correct them.

One lesson regarding our mistakes that can only be learned in the second mile is how devastating losing can actually be, and it can be the motivating factor that is necessary to push us on through the second mile to our victory.

Pete Sampras was once asked to name the most important tennis match he'd ever played at the U.S. Open. The four-time Open tennis champ chose the 1992 final, a match he'd actually lost to Stefan Edberg in a tough four-setter.

It was a terrible disappointment—one that most of us would choose to forget if it had happened to us. But Pete Sampras sees that loss as a major turning point in his career. As he explains, "Before that match, I didn't hate to lose." The bitterness of the loss provided Pete with the motivation he needed to get his game into full gear. It inspired him to discipline himself and give his best effort all the time. Before the Edberg match, Pete was a "one-hit wonder." Now—with thirteen Grand Slam titles to his credit, he's in the running for "Best Player in the History of the Game."[4] The second-mile, the place where second chances abound, propels us toward victory!

God is always willing and ready to give us a second chance. But one pitfall that causes many Christians to fall is that they often tend to seek the victory more than the One who gives them that victory. As you run the second mile and pursue the goals God sets for you, be sure to continually perform "priority checks" in your heart and mind. Which do you love more: God or the second chances He provides?

Kelly Williams faced a hard question when he was launching a new church start in Colorado Springs, Colorado. During the initial stages, the attendance fluctuated, but never exceeded a handful. One night, no one at all showed up, and Kelly faced the fact that he might not be cut out for church planting—that he could fail. As he flirted with quitting, he opened his Bible to John 10 and began to read Jesus' words about the Good Shepherd who lays down His life for His sheep.

As he read, Kelly clearly heard God's voice: "I know you are willing to be a success for Me, but are you willing to be a failure for Me? Are you willing to lay down your life for these sheep?" His open Bible opened his heart. "Yes, Lord, yes!" Kelly prayed. "I'll lay down my life for these sheep. If it is Your will, this is the hill I'll die on; I'll fight to the bitter end."[5]

Those who are willing to be a success for God are many. Those who are desperate for God and want Him even if it means being a "failure" are the blessed few. Kelly went on to establish a flourishing church, but the point is, he was willing to follow God's will for his life—wherever it took him. He surrendered his second mile to his God—and his God was able to take this surrender and make out of it something truly beautiful. Are you desperate for God today? Not desperate for His blessings; not desperate for success; but desperate for *Him*?

Sometimes running the second mile can mean not only receiving another chance for ourselves from God, but also extending a second chance to others around us. Perseverance in relationships will always require the extension of forgiveness. How willing are you to take this kind of risk with the people in your life?

The movie *Hoosiers* tells the almost-Cinderella-like story of a small-town Indiana high-school basketball team that wins the state championship. One important character, an alcoholic named Shooter, played by Dennis Hopper, has failed at most things in his life—but he has an extraordinary knowledge of and passion for the game of basketball.

The coach, played by Gene Hackman, works with Shooter to give him a second chance in life. He asks Shooter to be his assistant coach, and soon Shooter is on the bench.

The little-known Hickory High School basketball team is starting to experience winning ways when, during a pivotal game, the coach decides to get himself thrown out. He pulls the referee aside and says, "Take me out of the game." The ref doesn't know what the coach is up to, but he tosses him from the game.

Shooter is terrified. A few scenes earlier, after another drinking binge, Shooter promised the coach he'd stay sober and remain as the assistant on one condition: "You've got to give me your *word*," said Shooter, "that you will *not* be kicked out of no games!"

The end of the game is near, and the score is tied. The Hickory players call a timeout. In the team huddle, all eyes are on Shooter, including his son's, who never thought his dad should be in this position in the first place. Shooter is paralyzed by fear. He can't speak. Finally his son says, "You reckon number four will put up their last shot, Dad?" That seems to jumpstart Shooter, and he haltingly calls a play. The team goes back on the floor and begins to execute it when Shooter calls another timeout.

Now he is completely engaged in the game, and his knowledge and passion for basketball have overtaken his fear. He lays out the strategy for the next play with confidence: "All right, now listen to me. This is the last shot that we got. All right? We're gonna run the picket fence at 'em. Merle, you're the swing man. Jimmy, you're solo right. All right, Merle should be open swinging around the end of that fence. Now boys, don't get caught watchin' that paint dry!"

The players are with him. They walk back onto the floor, run the play to perfection, and sink the game-winning basket. Of course, Shooter and the players are deliriously happy. Amid the celebration, Shooter's son looks into his father's eyes and says, "You did good, Pop. You did real good."[6]

A weak, shame-filled alcoholic did "real good"

because the coach had decided he was worth taking a risk on. In the same way, God sees our value and loves us enough to take a risk on us. Are you taking this same kind of "second-chance risk" on the other people in your life who may need this kind of encouragement?

We were made to succeed—no matter what our past failures might have been. When we keep our eyes on our heavenly Father—and desire to know Him more than we desire the victory that He so graciously offers—we begin to walk the path of the second mile and see just what receiving a second chance is all about. When this happens, He will turn our failures into victory!

This happened in the life of well-known child psychologist and radio talk-show host James Dobson. In the early 1970s, concerned about the disintegration of the family and the increasing divorce rate, Dr. Dobson, who was a little-known psychologist in a southern California university hospital, wrote a book in support of corporal punishment: *Dare to Discipline.*

The popularity of this controversial volume caught the eye of TV talk-show guru Phil Donahue, who invited Dr. Dobson to appear on his Chicago-based show in 1978. Unfortunately, Donahue made the Ph.D. in child development look like a child himself. To this day, Dr. Dobson readily admits that his performance on Donahue's show was his worst ever. He left the set feeling like a total failure.

But Dr. Dobson's despair was short-lived. The next day, driven by his dismal performance, he sought out a 65-year-old advertising agent in a Chicago suburb to discuss the possibility of a national radio program. Doug Mains invited Dr. Dobson to his one-man studio in Wheaton, Illinois, where Dr. James Dobson proceeded to record the pilot broadcast of "Focus on the Family." What has developed from a disastrous television appearance is nothing short of mind-boggling. "Focus on the Family" is heard on more than 6,000 radio stations around the world, and the ten magazines the company now publishes reach 2.3 million families each month.[7]

What failures have consumed your life? How can you turn them into success wilder than you ever imagined? Place them in God's hands and see what He will do. You were made to soar!

I recently read a story that so clearly illustrates the second-mile principle of the second chance:

There was a farmer who had an incredible love of nature, particularly of wild animals. One day, while he was walking in the woods near his farm, he came across an injured baby eagle that had fallen out of its nest. Knowing it would be abandoned to die, he gathered it up and took it home.

The nurture and care the little eagle received from the farmer restored its health, and soon it spent the days sharing the barnyard with the chickens and turkeys. They ate together every day, and the eagle quickly grew to its full size—complete with a fifteen-foot wingspan.

The farmer had a friend who was a naturalist, and he agreed to come show the eagle how to fly. The two men stepped into the barnyard, and the naturalist picked up the eagle, gave him a toss into the wind, and said, "Fly!" But the eagle just jumped to the ground, joined the rest of the barnyard birds, and continued to peck at the food.

The farmer and the naturalist repeated this exercise many times over the next few days, always with the same results. But then the naturalist said, "I have an idea. Be ready tomorrow before dawn, and I will come and get you and the eagle."

The next morning the naturalist and the farmer took the eagle to the top of a nearby mountain just before dawn. The naturalist took the eagle and said, "You are an eagle; God made you to soar in His sky."

When he spoke those words, a beam of light hit the face of the eagle as the sun rose from behind the mountain. The eagle shuddered with what seemed like new life, then spread its wings, mounted the wind, and began to fly.

You and I are not unlike that eagle. Sometimes we have to get away from the chickens and the turkeys in order to do what we are called to do. But it is not always easy, especially if we have accepted our surroundings and measure ourselves by those who are content to just peck around in the barnyard of life. But God never called us to do what is easy; He has called us to spread our wings of faith and fly because we were made to soar.

Right now, you may feel like one of those chickens or turkeys. Perhaps you have made mistakes that you think have grounded you for life and you just don't know how you can even begin the second mile. The way to get out there is to just get into position—and go! Although the second mile may be significantly harder than the first to run, it is not nearly as crowded. God has already given you a second chance, so spread your wings of faith and begin to soar.

MILE MARKERS

➤ Have you ever needed a second chance from God? In what way? What was God's response?

➤ It has been said that "our greatest fear should not be of failure, but of succeeding at something that doesn't really matter." What does this statement mean to you?

➤ Does someone currently need a second chance from you? What could you do in order to give them that chance?

➤ Which is more important to you at this time in your life—God, or the victory He promises? Explain your answer.

➤ How can the mistakes you have made in your first mile become motivation for you in the second mile? (Be specific.)

The block of granite which was an obstacle in the path of the weak becomes a steppingstone in the path of the strong.
—Thomas Carlyle

Character cannot be developed in ease and quiet. Only through experience of trial and suffering can the soul be strengthened, vision cleared, ambition inspired, and success achieved.
—Helen Keller

Yet amid all these things we are more than conquerors and gain a surpassing victory through Him Who loved us.
—Romans 8:37 AMP

Jumping the Hurdles

So many people believe that after they become a Christian, life will suddenly become so much easier, and all of their problems will be solved. But Jesus never promised a life of ease—our final rest and greatest rewards will be given when we reach the end of our last race and we go to be with our Savior in heaven.

Until that time, we will face adversity—that's a guarantee! But we have an even greater promise concerning those obstacles and hurdles:

> *Yet amid all these things we are more than conquerors and gain a surpassing victory through Him Who loved us.*
>
> *For I am persuaded beyond doubt (am sure) that neither death nor life, nor angels nor principalities, nor things impending and threatening nor things to come, nor powers,*
>
> *Nor height nor depth, nor anything else in all creation will be able to separate us from the love of God which is in Christ Jesus our Lord.*
>
> —Romans 8:37–39 AMP

What a powerful promise! No matter what hurdles are in our path as we run our second-mile race, we will not only win, but we will be "more than conquerors"! Notice that Paul did not say that we would not face adversity—we may face things "impending" or "threatening"—but none of these things, not illness, not persecution, not family problems, or financial difficulties, can *ever* separate us from God's love. And He is the One who gives us the victory!

Once we understand that in the midst of our second-mile challenges lie great opportunities—and challenges—we need to know how to connect with the things God has made available for us, the things that will bring us the victory. We need to connect with God's miracles and second chances and then run our race in such a way as to be an example to others.

Imagine a truck equipped with a trailer hitch. That truck can be backed up to a trailer all day long, but unless someone knows how to connect the trailer to the ball on the truck, it's not going anywhere. The two are compatible, even designed to work together, just like miracles, second-chances, and being a living example are designed to work with us to bring about victory in our lives. But if we don't know how to connect them together, they can't be effective in our situation.

So, if God has already made these things available for us, what do we have to do to connect with them?

The secret is to *disconnect* from any circumstance or situation that conflicts with the race we are running. This could involve distressing circumstances, negative situations—or even conflicts with other people. These are just a few of the hurdles we must jump as we run the second mile.

In the book of Genesis, we find the story of a man named Jacob and his brother, Esau, who had a conflict due to something they had both done wrong when they were young men. Because Esau was the firstborn son, he was to receive the "birthright," meaning he was entitled to special blessings from his father. One day Esau came in from the field and was very hungry. Jacob had prepared a meal for himself, and because he had always used deceitful tactics in his life to get whatever he wanted, he followed the same pattern and offered Esau the food in exchange for his birthright. Esau's lack of respect for his birthright, combined with Jacob's greed, created an atmosphere of strife that eventually divided their respective families. Although Esau and Jacob both had a heritage filled with the promises of God, the weight of their conflict kept them from fully receiving those promises.

It is interesting to note that the name *Jacob* meant "to overthrow by tripping up; a conniver; a deceiver." Instead of just receiving the blessings of God that were already his, Jacob continued to resort to deceit to get them. That is, until one night when he had an encounter with a man who was later revealed to be an angel of God.

> *So Jacob was left alone, and a man wrestled with him till daybreak. When the man saw that he could not overpower him, he touched the socket of Jacob's hip so that his hip was wrenched as he wrestled with the man. Then the man said, "Let me go, for it is daybreak."*
>
> *But Jacob replied, "I will not let you go unless you bless me."*
>
> *The man asked him, "What is your name?"*
>
> *"Jacob," he answered.*
>
> *Then the man said, "Your name will no longer be Jacob, but Israel, because you have struggled with both God and human beings and have overcome."*
>
> —Genesis 32:24–28

You see, things were about to change in Jacob's life and God didn't want him running his second mile like he had run the first one, struggling with the conflict created by his own deceitful actions. He didn't want Jacob to even *think* like he thought before, so God changed his name to Israel, which meant "prince with God."

Now I am not suggesting that we all go change our names, but when we become born again we each become known as "Christian." And that new name, which becomes ours, is a reminder that *all things* have become new. We do not have to carry the burdens we used to carry, and we do not have to think the way we used to think. The Bible says it like this: *Cast all your anxiety on him because he cares for you* (1 Peter 5:7), and, *We take captive every thought to make it obedient to Christ* (2 Corinthians 10:5). Whenever we face the hurdles of adversity in our lives, we must cast our worry and anxiety onto the Lord, and then take care that the *negative situation* does not pull us down into *negative thinking.*

Jacob knew he had to settle the conflict with his brother, so he gathered his flocks of animals and had them herded in droves as a gift for Esau:

He [Jacob] *himself went on ahead and bowed down to the ground seven times as he approached his brother.*

But Esau ran to meet Jacob and embraced him; he threw his arms around his neck and kissed him. And they wept.

Esau asked, "What do you mean by all these droves I met? I already have plenty, my brother. Keep what you have for yourself."

"No, please!" said Jacob. "If I have found favor in your eyes, accept this gift from me. For to see your face is like seeing the face of God, now that you have received me favorably."

—Genesis 33:3–4, 8–10

Jacob ran the race, choosing to go the second mile by blessing his older brother rather than continuing to curse him, and in so doing, he successfully leaped the obstacle of conflict and ran toward victory in his circumstances.

This story of conflict resolution reminds me of what Brennan Manning had to say about the late Christian recording artist Rich Mullins:

Rich once taught me an invaluable lesson one day about the true meaning of repentance. One rainy day he got into a blistering argument with his road manager, Gay Quisenberry.

Angry words were hurled back and forth, and Rich stormed out the door. Early the following morning, Gay was awakened by a sound sleep by the loud buzz of a motor outside her house.

Groggily, she looked out the window and saw Rich mowing her lawn![1]

Not only did Rich Mullins face the conflict, but he chose resolution by taking the higher road, the path of the second mile.

Your own hurdle may or may not involve other people; perhaps it is a habit from which you just can't seem to break free, or maybe poor self-esteem due to someone else's behavior toward you. Whatever the case, the devil wants to use that obstacle to get you to think the way you used to think and do the things you used to do. Ultimately he wants you out of the race altogether.

No matter what hurdles you face in life, what obstacles you must overcome, God can bring good out of the situation, turn it around for His glory, and ultimately bring the victory.

Seven Chinese guards surrounded Gao Feng, who was handcuffed to a chair. The guards took turns shocking him with cattle prods. "Eat!" they commanded. "And we will stop."

Gao Feng had gone on a hunger strike to get back his copy of the Scriptures that the guards had taken from him. They were torturing him to get him to stop the hunger strike. At times, he thought he could no longer stand the pain, but he didn't give up. They never broke his spirit.

"You couldn't reason with the guards," Gao Feng said, "because they weren't human."

Gao Feng, a thirty-year-old worker at Chrysler's Jeep plant in Beijing, had tried to work within the Communist government system to get a Protestant church registered. Only government-sanctioned churches were legal in China—all others were illegal, their services often disrupted by the police, and the pastors and congregations were continually beaten and imprisoned for the stand they took for the gospel.

Gao Feng collected signatures for a petition seeking government registration for his church so that they could meet legally. It was for this "crime" that he was arrested and sent to prison without a trial, his home and possessions confiscated.

As a result of his hunger strike, Gao Feng was sent to a northern province for "re-education through labor." While there, he lived in a twelve-by-twenty-foot cell with sixteen other prisoners. They spent twelve hours each day working in the fields. At night, with so many people crammed into such a small cell, they had to arrange themselves a certain way so that everyone could lay down.

When he was transferred back to Beijing, he refused to chant the pro-government slogan with the other prisoners, so his "re-education" was continued. This time, his brainwashing included being forced to watch the news every evening on government-controlled television. Finally, after more than two years in prison and in re-education camps, Gao Feng was released on February 7, 1998.

The remarkable part of the story is Gao Feng's attitude toward the hurdles that he faced in his second-mile race: To him, all of the torture and brainwashing was worth it, and he declared that he would happily go to prison again if that is what God called him to do: "I would prefer to be in prison for two years than to do nothing for God," he said. In fact, he feels lucky for his experiences. As news of his situation reached believers in many countries, people wrote to the Chinese government demanding his release. Gao Feng says that the international attention focused on his case actually earned him better treatment from the Chinese authorities and shed light on the plight of Christians in that region of the world.[2]

Gao Feng's story is similar to that of many Christians throughout the centuries, believers who faced adversity and, with God's help, furthered the cause of the gospel and brought victory to God's kingdom.

In seventeenth-century England, John Bunyan also experienced imprisonment for the sake of the gospel, a hurdle that, because he faced it in strength and victory, God was able to use for His glory:

"I will let you go, if you promise not to preach." The judge looked down from his bench at John Bunyan.

"Sir," the Christian replied, "I will stay in prison till the moss grows on my eyelids rather than disobey God!"

"Then I hereby sentence you to six years in the Bedford jail."

God had given John Bunyan a powerful preaching gift and the great ability to touch the hearts of men. Although he wasn't well-educated—he had been forced to quit school at an early age to help his father work—he had been able to learn to read. While in prison, Bunyan read two books: the *King James Bible* and John Foxe's *Book of Martyrs*. He could not contain himself, and began to preach to his fellow prisoners. During this time, John Bunyan gained a new awareness of the truth of Scripture and of the presence of Jesus Christ, declaring: "Jesus Christ also was never more real and apparent than now: Here I have seen Him and felt Him indeed!"

During his imprisonment, he also began to write. He wrote many books and tracts, including the story of his conversion, *Grace Abounding to the Chiefest of Sinners*. As soon as he was released, John Bunyan started preaching again, and within just a few weeks, he was back in jail. Six years later, the King of England suspended the laws against the Nonconformists, and Bunyan was released.

By now, he was in great demand as a preacher. He frequently visited London, where he preached to large congregations. Sometimes as many as 1,200 people would attend a service at 7 o'clock on a winter morning. On Sundays, the meetinghouse could not hold all who wanted to hear him, and hundreds were turned away.

After three short years, the King of England changed his mind and began persecuting Nonconformists again. Bunyan was sent to jail for the third time. While in prison, this second-mile race-runner began writing a book that would help thousands of believers for centuries to come. *Pilgrim's Progress*, the first novel ever written, is the story of a dream in which Christian journeys from the City of Destruction to the Celestial City. Some have called it "the most excellent map to be found anywhere."

Today *Pilgrim's Progress* continues to be one of the best-known Christian books of all time and has been translated into hundreds of languages. And when China's Communist government (where Gao Feng's life had a tremendous impact) printed *Pilgrim's Progress* as an example of Western cultural heritage, an initial printing of 200,000 was sold out in three days![3]

Consider the following hymn written by John Bunyan, which clearly sets forth the principles of the person driven to run the second mile—no matter the hurdles, no matter the cost:

He who would valiant be 'gainst all disaster,
Let him in constancy follow the Master.
There's no discouragement shall make him once relent
His first avowed intent to be a pilgrim.

Since, Lord, Thou dost defend us with Thy Spirit,
We know we at the end shall life inherit.
Then fancies flee away! I'll fear not what men say,
I'll labor night and day to be a pilgrim.

—John Bunyan

God's plan is for you to connect with His miracles, His second chances, and the exemplary life that He has provided for you in Jesus Christ. The victory is yours, no matter what hurdles may stand in your path. The second mile is the place where you will begin to overcome the obstacles, to jump the hurdles, and to win the race—if you are willing to press on in those things that God has set before you. Jump the hurdles . . . victory awaits!

MILE MARKERS

> Edmund Burke once said, "He that wrestles with us strengthens our nerves, and sharpens our skill. Our antagonist is our helper." What do you think of this statement? How can the hurdles you face and overcome today help you in running the second mile tomorrow?

> What hurdles are you facing in your life right now? How can you begin to apply the principles discussed in this chapter to your situation?

> God loves to bring good out of each and every situation that His children face. Think of a time in your life when He brought good out of a seemingly hopeless situation. How can remembering what He has done in the past enable you to continue trusting Him in the future?

Perseverance is not a long race; it is many short races one after another.
—Walter Elliott

Go the extra mile. It's never crowded.
—Executive Speechwriter Newsletter

I consider my life worth nothing to me; if only I may finish the race and complete the task the Lord Jesus has given me.
—Acts 20:24

Getting Your Second Wind

Having been an average or mediocre long-distance runner in high school, then running halfway across America in 1990, I learned just what it was to get a second wind.

Second wind is a term runners use to describe an incredible experience the body undergoes at the point where their strength has run out. Something happens within the respiratory system that causes it to open up again just like it was brand new. It is an astonishing phenomenon that can only be fully appreciated by those who experience it.

God has not called any of us to run the second mile in an exhausted condition. He has called us to run the second mile full of life, strength, joy, peace, and all of the wonderful things that His Word wants us to experience. But in order to do so, we need to have a second-wind encounter.

The apostle Paul faced countless struggles and suffering throughout his race, but despite his difficulties, he wrote a number of encouraging letters to the early churches. In his letter to the Philippians, for example, written while he was a prisoner, Paul revealed the source of strength and life from which he drew his second wind. It was the *gospel*, which literally translated means the "good news."

I thank my God every time I remember you. In all my prayers for all of you, I always pray with joy because of your partnership in the gospel from the first day until now, being confident of this, that he who began a good work in you will carry it on to completion until the day of Christ Jesus.

It is right for me to feel this way about all of you, since I have you in my heart; for whether I am in chains or defending and confirming the gospel, all of you share in God's grace with me. God can testify how I long for all of you with the affection of Christ Jesus.

And this is my prayer: that your love may abound more and more in knowledge and depth of insight, so that you may be able to discern what is best and may be pure and blameless until the day of Christ, filled with the fruit of righteousness that comes through Jesus Christ—to the glory and praise of God.

Now I want you to know, brothers [and sisters], that what has happened to me has really served to advance the gospel. As a result, it has become clear throughout the whole palace guard and to everyone else that I am in chains for Christ. Because of my chains, most of the brothers [and sisters] *in the Lord have been encouraged to speak the word of God more courageously and fearlessly.*

Convinced of this, I know that I will remain, and I will continue with all of you for your progress and joy in the faith, so that through my being with you again your joy in Christ Jesus will overflow on account of me.

Whatever happens, conduct yourselves in a manner worthy of the gospel of Christ. Then, whether I come and see you or only hear about you in my absence, I will know that you stand firm in one spirit, contending as one man for the faith of the gospel. . . . For it has been granted to you on behalf of Christ not only to believe on him, but also to suffer for him, since you are going through the same struggle you saw I had.

—Philippians 1:3–14, 25–27, 29–30

At the time Paul wrote this letter, the gospel was brand new, and he had committed his life to explaining just what this good news was: Jesus Christ had come and made freedom from the law of sin and death available to all humanity.

Sadly, there are churches today that don't seem to understand that the gospel was, and still is, good news. They continue to preach a legalistic, religious message that does nothing but instill doubt, fear, and unbelief in those who hear it. When I was young, I attended a church just like that. All their negative messages did was scare me. But the gospel is not bad news—nothing about it is negative! The gospel of Jesus Christ is positive, and it always brings life, freedom, and liberty to all who hear it.

When we reach the place on our second mile where we need a refreshing second wind, the first thing we need to do is make sure that we are in a place where the good news of the gospel is being preached. If the gospel is not the central theme around which our church experience is based, then we can never tap in to three gospel-centered components that are revealed in Paul's message to the Philippians: the fellowship of the gospel, the furtherance of the gospel, and the faith of the gospel.

Fellowship that is based on the gospel is an essential element of gaining that precious second wind. Spending time engaging in negative conversation or negative encounters will literally knock the wind right out of us! God uses the refreshing fellowship of the gospel to give us a second wind.

The furtherance of the gospel brings about an increase of oxygen. The more we talk about the gospel, the more we further the good news. And because we are spreading the gospel, the oxygen of the Spirit will cause us to grow bigger on the inside.

Finally, there is the faith of the gospel. The Bible says that without faith it is impossible to please God. Faith that is grounded in the good news of Jesus Christ will always breathe fresh life into any second-mile runner.

God uses the fellowship of the gospel, the furtherance of the gospel, and the faith of the gospel to give us the second wind we need in order to complete our second mile. You may come from a background similar to mine in which you have heard nothing but legalistic, "religious" messages that all but suffocated the life of God that dwells within you. I can tell you from experience that the good news Paul first preached to the early church has not changed one bit. Jesus Christ has set you free from the law of sin and death. And it is the good news of the gospel that is about to breathe new life into you and cause you to experience your own second wind!

The Fellowship of the Gospel

It is wonderful to attend church, to be able to experience the presence of God and hear His Word. But there is another reason we attend church, and that is for fellowship.

Eric "The Swimmer" Moussambani of Equatorial Ghana was an unlikely hero of the Sydney Olympic Games. The twenty-two-year-old African had only learned to swim the previous January, had only practiced in a twenty-meter pool without lane markers, and had never raced more than fifty meters. By a special invitation of the International Olympic Committee, under a special program that permits poorer countries to participate even though their athletes don't meet customary standards, he had been entered in the 100-meter men's freestyle.

When the other two swimmers in the heat were disqualified because of false starts, Moussambani was forced to swim alone. Eric Moussambani was, to use the words of an Associated Press story about his race, "charmingly inept." He never put his head under the water's surface and flailed wildly to stay afloat. With ten meters left to the wall, he virtually came to a stop. Some spectators thought he might drown! Even though his time was over a minute slower than what qualified for the next level of competition, the capacity crowd at the Olympic Aquatic Center stood to their feet and cheered the swimmer on.

After what seemed like an eternity, the African reached the wall and hung on for dear life. When he had caught his breath and regained his composure, the French-speaking Moussambani said through an interpreter, "I want to send hugs and kisses to the crowd. It was their cheering that kept me going."[1]

Just like Eric Moussambani, we, too, need the crowd to "keep us going." We need like-minded believers around us to encourage us in the race we are running. It is so important to go to a church where we can enjoy the fellowship of people who share our convictions. I am convinced that Paul experienced a "fellowship of the gospel" that had become part of the core of his being. And it was this fellowship of the gospel that strengthened him and gave him the second wind he needed each time he faced hardship and controversy.

There are three statements Paul made in his letter to the Philippians that show us just how important the fellowship of the gospel was to him.

First, we know that Paul kept his Philippian brothers and sisters in the forefront of his mind because he wrote, *I thank my God every time I remember you* (Philippians 1:3).

I know that whenever I am away from my wife and children for any period of time, all I have to do when I feel discouraged is look at their photograph and I immediately experience a sense of encouragement in my soul. That's because our life is built around the gospel and when I think about them, God will always breathe life into me.

In Philippians 4:8–9, Paul wrote, *Finally, brothers [and sisters], whatever is true, whatever is noble, whatever is right, whatever is pure, whatever is lovely, whatever is admirable—if anything is excellent or praiseworthy—think about such things. Whatever you have learned or received or heard from me, or seen in me—put it into practice.*

Paul knew that whatever we allow our minds to think about is what will be planted in our spirits. In essence Paul was saying, "When I think of you I am encouraged. The thought of you enables me to be in chains without being discouraged, because I know you are out doing what I taught you to do. When I think of you, I think of the gospel and what you are doing for it." Paul's thoughts about the fellowship of the gospel gave him a second wind.

Like Paul, each of us needs to think about the fellowship of the gospel when we are going through tough times. Often, when we are running out of spiritual oxygen, God brings someone to mind with whom we share the fellowship of the gospel. Soon we find ourselves blessed and motivated by the encouragement that comes just from thinking about them.

Second, we know that Paul kept these people in his heart because he wrote, *It is right for me to feel this way about all of you, since I have you in my heart* (Philippians 1:7). We can have people in our thoughts, but when they are in our hearts, they have become part of the fabric of who we are.

That is what God wants in the body of Christ. He wants us to be so woven together that when one member of the body hurts, we all hurt, and when one member rejoices, we all rejoice. If we want to get our second wind, then we must begin to feel what the body of Christ is feeling. We must begin to feel the heartbeat of God in His body. When we do, it is no longer a thought—it is a feeling.

I may have to make myself a note when I have an appointment with the dentist because it is not something that is in my heart. But Christianity is not like a dentist appointment. I don't have to remind myself to pray for the people with whom I have fellowship because they are in my heart.

The fellowship of the gospel is so strong that we are empowered and illuminated even when we just think about it. And when we keep this fellowship in our heart, we can feel it breathing life into us—right when we need that second wind. Paul was so connected to his brothers and sisters through the fellowship of the gospel that although he was imprisoned, he felt free.

Third, Paul wrote that he kept those with whom he had fellowship in his prayers: *And this is my prayer: that your love may abound more and more in knowledge and depth of insight* (Philippians 1:9).

Whenever someone is in our thoughts and in our heart, they will automatically be in our prayers. Too often, we make prayer legalistic and rigid. We struggle to come up with "just the right words" for our spouses, families, and other loved ones. But once we allow those people who are in our thought life to gain entrance into our hearts, they are almost automatically going to be a loving part of our prayers.

Whenever someone is woven into our hearts and we begin to pray for them, we are going to experience what they are feeling. That little bit of pain we experience when we pray is not God punishing us; it is His way of showing us how to pray for them. As we begin to lift them up, God will lift us up. And any time we make someone else a part of us and we pray for them, we get to experience the joy of their victory.

The Bible says, *Let us not give up meeting together, as some are in the habit of doing, but let us encourage one another* (Hebrews 10:25). That was never intended to be a legalistic statement. What it is telling us is that we need the fellowship of the gospel; we need the good news; we need to be around people who love Christ as much as we love Him. That is what fellowship is.

Some people wonder how I can preach six sermons each and every week. I can do it because my entire life is built around the gospel. And it is the fellowship of the gospel that I receive both at church and at home that gives me the second wind I need to do what God has called me to do.

God has called you to do something, too. Whether you are answering that call in the business world, through volunteer involvement, or at home raising children, God wants the fellowship of the gospel to be a vital part of everything you do. If you haven't already done so, find a church where you can be around other Christians who love Jesus and begin to experience the benefits of the fellowship of the gospel.

The Furtherance of the Gospel

On June 28, 1776, at seventy-three years of age, John Wesley related in his journal that he was far more able to preach than he had been at age twenty-three. In the course of his ministry, he had traveled more than 4,000 miles a year (giving him exercise and a "change of air"), made a practice of getting up at four o'clock every morning, and was able to go to sleep immediately every night. In his entire lifetime, he never lost a night's sleep, experienced four illnesses that, according to his journal, actually served to "invigourate" him, and he wrote about possessing what he called "evenness of temper": "I feel and grieve; but, by the grace of God, I fret at nothing."[2] John Wesley had caught his second wind—and he directly attributed his strength and vitality late in his lifetime to the work he had done in spreading the gospel!

The furtherance of the gospel is a vital part of the second wind we each need in order to run a victorious race. Just prior to Jesus' death, as He was explaining to His disciples the signs that would come at the end of the age, He said, *"The gospel must first be preached to all nations"* (Mark 13:10). Following His resurrection, He appeared to the eleven and said to them, *"Go into all the world and preach the good news* [gospel] *to all creation"* (Mark 16:15).

Paul understood that it was the furtherance of the gospel—not money, status, or position—that would open the door to a joy-filled, abundant life. He knew that it didn't matter what people thought of him or even if he was in prison—which was just where he was when he wrote these words: *Now I want you to know, brothers* [and sisters], *that what has happened to me has really served to advance the gospel* (Philippians 1:12). He went on to write, *And because of this I rejoice. Yes, and I will continue to rejoice, for I know that through your prayers and the help given by the Spirit of Jesus Christ, what has happened to me will turn out for my deliverance* (verses 18–19). It was the furtherance of the gospel that caused the air of heaven and the wind of God to blow through his life.

At Victory Church, we have always made the furtherance of the gospel our number-one goal. We want to reach as many people as we can, because we know how much God loves them and wants them to hear the good news. Our vision is to reach a city, change a nation, and touch the world with the gospel of Jesus Christ. And because of our commitment to that vision, God has enabled us to reach untold thousands worldwide through television, live Internet broadcasts, and publications.

Due to the number of people who have been touched by the gospel over the past few years, our church has experienced tremendous growth. We are now in our fourth auditorium and have planted, or helped to plant, three other churches in different cities. The buildings we have built were not just for those of us who are already here. They were built for every lost and dying soul that our church would encounter. They were built to bring furtherance to the gospel, and as we do it, the breath of God continues to flow in our midst.

Any time we are involved in the furtherance of the gospel, we are going to develop an enthusiastic interest in serving others. In Paul's letter to the Romans, he wrote: *I am so eager to preach the gospel also to you who are at Rome. I am not ashamed of the gospel, because it is the power of God for the salvation of everyone who believes* (Romans 1:15–16). Jesus Christ clearly came first in Paul's life, and the welfare of others came next. His own feelings and what people thought of him just did not matter.

Those of us who have grown up in America have had the opportunity to experience God's blessings without fear of imprisonment. Because we are so used to being blessed, as a nation we have come to develop what I call a "me-mentality." Many people are more interested in serving their own purposes than in serving others.

During a recent flight, I was seated next to the CFO of a national fast-food chain, and I had the opportunity to talk with him about this observation. In his type of business, it is not uncommon to see people go to the counter to place an order with a server who treats them as if they were a nuisance. It's as though the customer has to become the servant to the person behind the cash register just to place an order.

Now this CFO knew that in order to be successful in a highly competitive market, his chain had to offer more than just good food. They had to offer superior customer service in a welcoming environment that would make their customers want to come back again and again. Their employees understood that the reason they had a job was because of the customers they served. The customer came first.

There is no place in the furtherance of the gospel for a "me-mentality." Any time we are involved in God's work, our motive must always be the best interest of others.

Putting ourselves last is not something that comes naturally. We each have to make that choice—often many times each day. The reason Paul was able to live a lifestyle of being last was because he understood that he had been bought at a price (see 1 Corinthians 6:19–20). He made a choice daily to die to himself, to live for Christ, and to serve others through the furtherance of the gospel.

Many people have the attitude of "I'm already pulled in so many different directions with the activities of life. There's no way I can afford adding the furtherance of the gospel to what I have to do." But the truth is, they can't afford not to! Any time we re-prioritize our lives, making the furtherance of the gospel our number-one goal, God is going to make sure that all of our own needs are met. He will make sure we have enough time, enough resources, and enough help to do what He has called us to do. That is because the furtherance of the gospel always causes the fresh wind of God to come into our lives.

I have seen this happen over and over again at Victory Church. Just about the time we develop a level of comfort in what we are doing, God enlarges the vision in a way that, without a second wind and His involvement, we would never reach the new goal.

You may have already come a long way in your race, and you may be feeling the need for a second wind. Right now, decide to make the furtherance of the gospel your number-one priority. When you do, you will experience the incredible spiritual second wind that God has made available to you through Jesus Christ.

The Faith of the Gospel

Once the fellowship of the gospel and the furtherance of the gospel have become a part of our lives, we realize that we are not running our race alone. We never again have to face challenges and hardship in an isolated and powerless position because of the faith of the gospel.

Paul wrote: *Whatever happens, conduct yourselves in a manner worthy of the gospel of Christ. Then, whether I come and see you or only hear about you in my absence, I will know that you stand firm in one spirit, contending as one man for the faith of the gospel* (Philippians 1:27).

The reason Paul could have faith in the face of his own challenges and hardships was because he had already experienced the fellowship of the gospel and was committed to the furtherance of the gospel. Apparently he knew exactly what his Philippian brothers and sisters were facing because he wrote: *You are going through the same struggle you saw I had* (Philippians 1:30). That is why he told them to stand firm in one spirit and strive together in one accord. Paul was saying, "Let's stand as though we are one person, unified in the faith of the gospel."

As a pastor, I realize that the local church is made up of many people who are at different stages of their development as Christians. They don't all have the same level of strength and faith. Like a single snowflake, they can be extremely frail. But if enough of these fragile snowflakes stick together, they can actually stop traffic!

Any time the body of Christ sticks together, we are going to stop the traffic of hell from running over our families. We are going to stop the traffic of hell from destroying our jobs and causing us to be depressed. The reason we can do this is because we stick together.

God established this principle of teamwork and faithfulness to one another as a means of rewarding Israel's obedience: *If you follow my decrees and are careful to obey my commands . . . five of you will chase a hundred, and a hundred of you will chase ten thousand, and your enemies will fall by the sword before you* (Leviticus 26:3, 8). In Ecclesiastes 4:12, we read, *Though one may be overpowered, two can defend themselves. A cord of three strands is not quickly broken.*

Jesus revealed the power behind this principle when He said to His disciples, *"I tell you the truth, whatever you bind on earth will be bound in heaven, and whatever you loose on earth will be loosed in heaven. Again, I tell you that if two of you on earth agree about anything you ask for, it will be done for you by my Father in heaven. For where two or three come together in my name, there am I with them"* (Matthew 18:18–20).

The reason we have so much power when we stick together is because we are coming into agreement with God's Word. And when two or more of us come together in agreement, Jesus said that He would be right there with us. That puts us on the winning side!

Paul understood that whenever believers are united through agreement in the faith of the gospel, they will always be victorious. He wrote: *I will know that you stand firm in one spirit, contending as one man for the faith of the gospel without being frightened in any way by those who oppose you. This is a sign to them that they will be destroyed, but that you will be saved—and that by God* (Philippians 1:27–28).

What Paul was telling his brothers and sisters was that they could know the outcome of the game ahead of time—they were going to win! Isn't it just like God to say, "No matter what you are going through, at the end of the race, you are going to cross the finish line, and you are going to win!" Isn't it nice that through the faith of the gospel, we can know ahead of time that we are winners?

If we, as believers, will just stand together in the faith of the gospel, we will have all the spiritual oxygen we need to live victoriously on this side of heaven. We don't have to run out of air, stamina—or faith.

Through the faith of the gospel, Paul was able to consider his imprisonment as a privilege because while he was in chains, the gospel was multiplying. Most people who become incarcerated feel an immediate, horrible sense of futility that causes them to withdraw like a tortoise into its shell. But this was not the case with Paul. Instead he rose up and encouraged people from his prison cell. He could do this because through the fellowship of the gospel and his commitment to further the gospel, he had developed the kind of faith that provided him with his second wind.

Like Paul, you may be facing a second-mile challenge today. You may feel imprisoned by your circumstances and see no way out. I am not suggesting that you need to suffer, but I want you to know that when you do suffer persecution, you can do what Paul did and say, "I am going to use this in my favor, and the gospel is going to be multiplied."

Get other believers with whom you share the fellowship of the gospel to stand in agreement with you for God's solution. As you come together, standing as one in the faith of the gospel, you will experience the second wind you need to go on and finish your race. And the best news is that God has already said that you are going to win!

MILE MARKERS

➢ How has fellowship with other believers made a difference in the race you are running? How have they hindered or encouraged you in the faith?

➢ How great of a priority is spreading the gospel in your life today? What changes could you make to place God and His will for your life at the center of your plans?

➢ In what areas do you need a "second wind" today? Begin to ask God for the faith you need to persevere in the race, and to run it with victory.

*Since Jesus went through every-
thing you're going through and
more, learn to think like him.*
—1 Peter 4:1 THE MESSAGE

*Christ is your example.
Follow in his steps.*
—1 Peter 2:21 NLT

*Let us fix our eyes on Jesus, the
author and perfecter of our faith.*
—Hebrews 12:2

Learning From Jesus

The finish line. The cheering crowds. One of the most critical points in any race is the time when the runner is approaching the finish line and begins to hear the praises of the people there to see him win. Crowds always assemble at the end of the course, pushing and shoving for the best position, because they want to watch the winner cross the finish line.

Jesus, our Coach throughout this race of life that we run, provides the example we need of how to finish successfully—how to run the second mile and win the race that God has set forth for us to run. Most coaches have played in the sport they coach; it's rare to find a tennis coach who has not played tennis himself, or a basketball coach who has never sunk any hoops in a game of his own. In the same way, Jesus, our Coach, ran the most successful race ever run, but He remembers the struggles and pitfalls He experienced—and He can help us face these challenges, if we listen to Him and follow His example.

Jesus' second-mile race began in His journey to the cross. In the book of Matthew, we read the account of the day Jesus entered Jerusalem, just prior to the appointed time of His death. This story is often referred to as The Triumphal Entry.

As they approached Jerusalem and came to Bethphage on the Mount of Olives, Jesus sent two disciples, saying to them, "Go to the village ahead of you, and at once you will find a donkey tied there, with her colt by her. Untie them and bring them to me. If anyone says anything to you, tell him that the Lord needs them, and he will send them right away."

This took place to fulfill what was spoken through the prophet: "Say to the Daughter of Zion, 'See, your king comes to you, gentle and riding on a donkey, on a colt, the foal of a donkey.'"

The disciples went and did as Jesus had instructed them. They brought the donkey and the colt, placed their cloaks on them, and Jesus sat on them. A very large crowd spread their cloaks on the road, while others cut branches from the trees and spread them on the road. The crowds that went ahead of him and those that followed shouted, "Hosanna to the Son of David!" "Blessed is he who comes in the name of the Lord!" "Hosanna in the highest!"

When Jesus entered Jerusalem, the whole city was stirred and asked, "Who is this?"

The crowds answered, "This is Jesus, the prophet from Nazareth in Galilee."

—Matthew 21:1–11

This story took place on what we now call Palm Sunday, the Sunday before Jesus was crucified. Jesus was just five days away from finishing His second mile. It is important to remember that this was the race He had chosen to run, not the race He was required to run by law.

This was a very crucial time for Jesus because—like in any race—when a runner approaches the finish line, that is where the people gather. The crowd that assembled to welcome Jesus was not just made of curiosity seekers. They included people whose lives had been forever changed because they came into contact with Him. In addition to the disciples, there were people in the crowd who were among the thousands that were fed with just a few fish and several loaves of bread. There were many who had been healed, and possibly those who had been raised from the dead. And there were others to whom He had said, "Your sins are forgiven," setting them free from the bondage of sin.

As Jesus entered Jerusalem that day, He was met by a crowd of people who were so enthusiastic that the entire city was stirred. At that point, it would have been so much easier for Him to take His eyes off the finish line and just quit while He was ahead, than to go through what He would experience over the next five days.

Throughout the race of life, God is going to call on each of us a number of times to accomplish something more than we think we are capable of doing. And each time we near the finish line, we will be tempted to say, "I am coming to the end of this thing, and I'm tired," and then cease to continue giving it all we've got. In order to finish each leg of our race victoriously, there are three things that we must learn from the way Jesus ran His second mile:

- First, Jesus used prophecy as a mile marker.
- Second, Jesus ran through the parade.
- Third, Jesus ran through the praise.

Imagine this crowd through the eyes of Jesus. That day, when they were asked who He was, they answered, "This is Jesus, the prophet from Nazareth in Galilee." They did not yet recognize Him as the Son of God, so the parade they created in order to give Him praise was because they esteemed Him as a prophet, not as the Messiah.

You may never experience a situation that in reality places you in the midst of an excited crowd of people as you run toward a finish line. But any time you are involved in doing something with and for God, I can guarantee that you will have to deal with prophecy, parades, and praise. As you learn how Jesus ran His second mile, you, too, will be able to handle the things you have to face as you run your race and finish in victory.

Jesus Used Prophecy as a Mile Marker

In 2000, *The Futurist* magazine catalogued some of the worst predictions of all time:

> "Inventions have long since reached their limit, and I see no hope for further developments."
> —Roman engineer
> Julius Sextus Frontinus, A.D. 100

> "The abdomen, the chest, and the brain will forever be shut from the intrusion of the wise and humane surgeon."
> —John Eric Erickson,
> surgeon to Queen Victoria, 1873

"Law will be simplified [over the next century]. Lawyers will have diminished, and their fees will have been vastly curtailed."

—journalist Junius Henri Browne, 1893

"It would appear we have reached the limits of what it is possible to achieve with computer technology."

—computer scientist
John von Neumann, 1949

"The Japanese don't make anything the people of the United States would want."

—Secretary of State
John Foster Dulles, 1954

"By the turn of the century, we will live in a paperless society."

—Roger Smith,
chairman of General Motors, 1986

"I predict the Internet . . . will go spectacularly supernova and in 1996 catastrophicallly collapse."

—Bob Metcalfe, *Infoworld*, 1995[1]

Aren't you glad that your faith isn't grounded in the predictions of man, but in the solid truth of God's Word? God has graced His Church with the gift of prophecy, and this is a valid and useful tool that should be used by God's people to further God's kingdom in the world. But in contemporary Christian culture, we have developed a troubling tendency to be directed by personal prophecy rather than being led by the Holy Spirit Himself.

I am certainly not against prophecy, but I believe that it can be dangerously misused when people are directed by it—and only it. Prophecy is for *confirmation*, and should be used cautiously for *direction*. We know that Jesus was not directed by prophecy, because He said, "I do nothing but what I see the Father do" (see John 5:19). For Jesus, prophecy was a mile marker, and that is exactly what God intends it to be for us.

Zechariah prophesied that Jesus would enter Jerusalem on Palm Sunday, riding on a donkey: *See, your king comes to you, righteous and having salvation, gentle and riding on a donkey, on a colt, the foal of a donkey* (Zechariah 9:9).

Jesus didn't look at this one prophecy and decide, *I'm through now because here I am riding on this donkey and here everybody is all happy and excited.* He didn't alter the plan of God for the sake of prophecy. Instead, He used it as a mile marker, knowing that there were still more prophecies to be fulfilled. Isaiah had prophesied, *Surely he took up our infirmities and carried our sorrows, yet we considered him stricken by God, smitten by him, and afflicted. But he was pierced for our transgressions, he was crushed for our iniquities* (Isaiah 53:4–5).

Jesus had to look beyond Zechariah to Isaiah, and finally to what He had prophesied about Himself: *The Son of Man is going to be betrayed into the hands of men. They will kill him, and on the third day he will be raised to life* (Matthew 17:22–23).

The first thing we need to learn about Jesus as He ran His second mile is that He did not allow prophecy to direct Him; He used it as a mile marker.

Some time during the 1980s, a book was published that gave 88 reasons why Jesus would return in 1988. I don't mean to be critical of the book, which was based on 88 biblical principles that were intended to help us, but that one book caused many people, both Christians and non-Christians, to alter their lives based on a prophetic word.

In America, it seems that there are two tendencies when we hear a word like that. One is that some believers get excited and take their focus off of the mission and the mandates of God. In 1988, there were probably people who actually believed that they were not going to be here much longer and went out and charged their credit cards to the limit.

Then there are those who hear such a prophecy and are immediately filled with fear: "Oh, I just don't know what is going to become of us. Things are growing darker day by day, and it's only going to get worse and worse!" I'm not just talking about lost people saying things like this; Christians do it, too.

It was just a few years ago that the entire world waited with an uneasy anticipation concerning what would happen at midnight when we entered the new millennium. We all heard the stories about how our bank accounts would be depleted and there would be no food because the trucking industry would come to a halt. Believers started negotiating and trying to determine what was going to happen. There were even individuals who dug water wells, bought generators, and stored up astronaut food to ensure their survival.

Any time we alter our lives because of a prophecy, instead of using it as a mile marker, we open the door for the devil to steal our strength and the reason for our existence, which is the furtherance of the gospel. Whether we allow a prophecy to create excitement or fear, the result is the same: It takes our eyes off of the true finish line, and it can even stop us from finishing the race.

Jesus did not allow prophecy to distract Him and keep Him from completing His race. He knew that He was on His second mile, so He saw those prophecies as mile markers and signs of the times—but He did not alter the plan of God or stop running.

There are many people today who are "predicting" things. All one needs to do to hear the latest version of how bad things are is to turn on the television and watch one of the many news programs that run twenty-four hours a day. They will give us plenty of reasons to think that Jesus is coming back before the end of this week.

Here is a prophetic word we can truly hang our hats on: Jesus will come back at the exact time God has set for Him to come back! Jesus said, *"You will hear of wars and rumors of wars, but see to it that you are not alarmed. Such things must happen, but the end is still to come"* (Matthew 24:6).

Every one of us knows that there have been rumors of trouble that have been floating around for a long, long time—forever, actually. These rumors are the alarms of the devil, intended to cause us to panic, to react in fear. But Jesus tells us to not be alarmed. When we allow what we hear to make us afraid, we take our focus off of what we have been called to do.

The Bible says that the purpose of prophecy is to strengthen, encourage, and comfort people—not to bring fear. It also tells us that those who prophesy actually edify the Church (see 1 Corinthians 14).

Perhaps your church background includes a religious message that made you fearful. Or maybe you have taken your focus off of what God called you to do when you became excited about a personal word of prophecy. In either case, there is only one thing you need to do: Turn that prophecy from a distraction into a second-mile marker, just like Jesus did. When you do, you will realize that you are closer to your finish line than you ever imagined.

Jesus Ran through the Parade

Glory is not always what it's cracked up to be. Consider one of Los Angeles's newest building, the Walt Disney Concert Hall, Frank Gehry's landmark $274 million creation of shimmering stainless steel. It is a beautiful sight to behold—if you don't have to live next to it.

Residents of a condominium facing the structure agree that their view is glorious, but the glory becomes overpowering when the sun begins to shine at midday. Portions of the gleaming concert hall reflect brilliantly into the windows of the condominium, and soon, the temperature rises as much as 15 degrees, forcing residents to come in off of their patios, draw the blinds, and turn on the air conditioner, at least until the sunlight shifts.

"You couldn't even see, and then the furniture would get really hot," one woman who lived on the fourth floor commented. "You would have to literally close the drapes, and you'd still feel the warmth in the house."

As the officials at the Disney building look for a way to dull the glare, they draped mesh blankets down the side of the glorious building to tone it down. This diminished the problem, but the effect was less than magnificent: Everyone who has seen it agrees that the building looks worse than it would have looked if had simply been built as a "normal" skyscraper.[2]

Sometimes the glory of man is disappointing. Sometimes it is fickle, and although tempting, it should never cause us to look away from the race God has called us to run.

Just imagine the scene as Jesus entered Jerusalem that Palm Sunday. He was riding on a donkey, and there were crowds of people that went ahead of Him and more who followed behind. The Bible says that many people laid their cloaks on the road and others cut branches and placed them in His path. They were having a parade.

Even though the people were having a good time, rejoicing as Jesus came to town, *their parade ended up being a charade.* The reason is that they did not yet fully know that Jesus was the Messiah. When the people of the city asked the parade-goers who Jesus was, they answered, *"This is Jesus, the prophet from Nazareth in Galilee"* (Matthew 21:11).

The parade was honoring Jesus as a man of God,

not the Son of God. And as it turned out, many of the people who were shouting "Hosanna" on Palm Sunday were shouting "Crucify Him!" by the following Friday.

Jesus understood their excitement and did not chastise anyone that day. But what we need to understand is that Jesus was not through running His race because He had not yet been to the cross.

The people were excited because they had seen Him raise the dead and feed the multitude, but those were just mile markers. Jesus had something far better to give them: forgiveness and everlasting life for all who called upon His name. Jesus knew about the parade.

The trouble with our culture is that we often celebrate prematurely. I have seen football players start celebrating at the five-yard line, only to have the ball knocked loose before they cross the goal line.

Jesus had something to say about these kinds of inappropriate responses: *"How can I account for this generation?"* He asked. *"The people have been like spoiled children whining to their parents, 'We wanted to skip rope, and you were always too tired; we wanted to talk, but you were always too busy.' John came fasting and they called him crazy. I came feasting and they called me a lush, a friend of the riff-raff. Opinion polls don't count for much, do they? The proof of the pudding is in the eating"* (Matthew 11:17–19 THE MESSAGE). You can't always please the crowd, He was saying. You may need to press past the parade, past the opinion polls, to continue running your second mile.

As Christians, we must always look ahead and press forward to do what God has called us to do. There are still countless thousands of people in this world who need to meet Jesus. Celebrations are great, but only if we have them in the right place and for the right reason. *Just don't let the party become a distraction to your race.*

As Jesus continued to run His second mile, He ran right through the parade. Although He was surrounded by a multitude of people who were shouting, "Hosanna!" and "Blessed is he who comes in the name of the Lord," He did not allow the parade to cause Him to celebrate prematurely. These people were celebrating because of what He had already done, but Jesus knew He still had to go to the cross. The reason Jesus didn't stop to celebrate history at that time was because He knew He was on His way to celebrate the future.

In order to run past the parade, Jesus had to be able to handle two specific challenges that were part of what was going on that day. It's what I call "pre-cross hype." The first thing Jesus had to overcome was the debate that was going on about who He really was. Was Jesus the prophet from Nazareth or was He really the Son of God? And second, He had to face the controversy between the people who expressed their worship by laying down their cloaks and palm branches and the legalists who detested this expression of praise.

Both of these challenges still exist today. Many people throughout the world, including those who are part of organized religions, will acknowledge that Jesus was a great prophet, but they argue that He is not the Son of God. And we don't even have to leave this country to encounter controversy about what is the appropriate way to express our faith. Let's look at how Jesus handled these challenges.

Because He had internal security and confidence in Himself and His mission, Jesus did not let external controversy affect Him. He knew who He was in the Father; therefore, He did not need the crowd's validation. Jesus was not arrogant or disrespectful as He ran through the parade because He did not have to look for the approval of men.

It took me a long time to learn this lesson. I spent a number of years looking for the approval of others to validate my move from alcoholism and drug use to my service of God. I was burning the candle at both ends trying to be a good husband, a good employee, and a good student as I prepared for the ministry. Then I realized that the only validation any of us need is from God alone. When we are born again, we have been bought with a price. So, whether I succeed or fail at anything I do, I am a success because I have found Christ. We all long to hear the words, "Well done ... good race!" but we don't need to hear them from the crowd that surrounds us; we need to hear them from God.

Now don't misunderstand what I am saying: There is nothing wrong with people affirming and encouraging each other, but that should be just the icing on the cake for us. Jesus' approval is the substance. Jesus knew that the affirmation of man was not His ultimate end. He was looking to the cross, the place where He would shed His blood for the sins of all humanity. He had determined that neither prophecy nor the parade was going to stop Him from finishing His race.

What about you? You may be doing the same thing I did a number of years ago. You may be so driven by the desire for validation that you have almost worn yourself out physically, spiritually, and emotionally. Maybe a lot of time and effort has been spent trying to conform to someone else's expectations about how you should express your faith in God. Perhaps you are so motivated by the need for people to affirm and encourage you, that without it you find it difficult to serve the Lord.

The good news is that you can be free from the weight of these challenges right now. Your life has already been bought by God, who paid the price with the life of His Son. And that is all the validation you need to seal your commitment to follow Him anywhere He wants you to go. Make the decision today not to be slowed down or stopped by the challenges you encounter on the second mile. When you do, you will run right through the parade and on to victory!

Jesus Ran Past the Praise

Following the attack on Pearl Harbor, Commander Joe Rochefort broke Japenese communication codes. Stationed at an intelligence base in Oahu, he predicted that the Japanese would attack Midway on June 3, 1942—which they did. Because of Rochefort's expertise, the United States surprised the Japanese Navy with its first defeat in 350 years. Japan lost four carriers, one cruiser, 2,500 men, 322 aircraft, and their best pilots. Due to the crippling defeat, Japan eventually lost the war.

But surprisingly, Rochefort never received recognition for his efforts. Instead, some intelligence men in Washington, D.C., took the credit, even though they themselves had actually predicted a June 10 date of attack. Washington sealed the records for forty years, and the mistake was not discovered until after that time. Rochefort was never properly rewarded; in fact, he was actually removed from intelligence and assigned to a floating dry dock in San Francisco.

But praise wasn't what Joe Rochefort was after. In their book *Deceit at Pearl Harbor*, Lieutenant Commander Ken Landis, Staff Sergeant Rex Gunn, and Sergeant Robert Andrade (all retired) wrote about a note Joe Rochefort always kept on his desk: "We Can Accomplish Anything, Providing No One Cares Who Gets the Credit." The authors declare, "That was the attitude that won the battle of Midway."[3]

The praise of man is fickle—what really matters is

what God thinks of what you do, especially as you run your second mile. When Jesus ran through the parade, He didn't just run past the cheering crowd that had gathered that day, He ran right on past the praise. Please don't misunderstand me: It was good that so many people were praising Jesus, but remember, at that point in time, Jesus had not yet been to the cross. Our celebration of Christ is what keeps us going and keeps us from stopping. Celebration should be what serves to rally us to the finish (see Philippians 1:6).

Each year, Victory Church produces and presents an Easter Illustrated Sermon filled with music, dance, and special effects. This vivid illustration of the extent to which God went in order to redeem humanity draws between twelve and fifteen thousand spectators annually. Over the Easter weekend, scores of men, women, and children either receive Jesus Christ for the first time or recommit their lives to Him.

As wonderful as those events are because of the lives that have been touched, we always keep in mind that they are nothing more than mile markers. We don't come together after the audience has gone home and the set is dismantled and say, "Hallelujah! Just look at what we did!" No, we keep right on going because the weekend after Easter is coming up and there are still people who are dying and going to hell, and people who need to be discipled. There is no "cruise control" on the journey to the cross, and there is no time for any of us to coast to our destiny! People who are without Christ don't have time for us to have a charade parade or a premature celebration.

Most of us are familiar with what is commonly called Jesus' Parable of the Ten Minas, found in the book of Luke. It illustrates the principle that we are to be actively involved in the things God has given us to do until Jesus returns.

A man of noble birth went to a distant country to have himself appointed king and then to return. So he called ten of his servants and gave them ten minas. "Put this money to work," he said, "until I come back."

He was made king, however, and returned home. Then he sent for the servants to whom he had given the money, in order to find out what they had gained with it.

The first one came and said, "Sir, your mina has earned ten more." The second came and said,

"Sir, your mina has earned five more."

—Luke 19:12–13, 15–16, 18

The king commended both of the servants, and as a result of their faithful and trustworthy service, gave each of them authority over a number of cities in his kingdom. Then a third servant came and returned the very same mina he had been given, which he had kept safely laid away in a piece of cloth. The king was displeased with the servant and said, *"Why then didn't you put my money on deposit, so that when I came back, I could have collected it with interest?" Then he said to those standing by, "Take his mina away from him and give it to the one who has ten minas"* (Luke 19:23–24).

While most of the king's minas were multiplying in the hands of faithful servants, one led a benign existence in the hands of a man who might have even been having a premature celebration to celebrate his good fortune at receiving the equivalent of 100 days' wages.

The same thing still happens today. It is always wonderful to watch churches prosper and grow to the point that we need larger buildings to accommodate all of the people who are involved in God's work. But sadly, this is often the very point at which many churches fail and die. We start celebrating too early, and while they are busy having a praise party, there are people who are walking off the supernatural cliff into hell.

I don't mean to be critical, but the reality is that we must move beyond today's victory—whether it is a building, an event, or the praise of people—and go on to complete the race.

To be clear, I am certainly not against the praise of people. We ought to be nice to each other and compliment each other when we do well, but praise is incomplete without crossing the finish line of destiny and eternity. If we are not careful, praise will put a coating on us that can cause us to lose our sensitivity to lost and hurting people. We should never let praise stop us from leading others to the Savior.

The only way we can successfully run past the praises of other people is to become actively involved in praising God. When we begin to focus on God's goodness and what Jesus has done for us, it begins to bring a proper alignment, or focus, to our daily lives and our praise.

You may never be in the position to literally run through a crowd, hearing shouts of praise as you move toward a victory. But the praise of people can be just as distracting coming from a few well-meaning friends. The way to run past the praise is to focus on what Jesus did just for you when He went to the cross. When you do, you will be able to move beyond the first-round victory of today and go on to complete the race.

MILE MARKERS

- Has prophecy ever been a "mile marker" for you? Did you use it as confirmation or as direction? What happened?

- Have you ever celebrated a victory prematurely, only to discover there was more still to be accomplished? What kept you from becoming discouraged at that point?

- How has the praise of other people been a distraction or an encouragement in your life? How can this praise motivate you to continue running the second mile?

- Which of these three examples that Jesus set for us—using prophecy as a mile marker; running through a parade; and running through praise— has the most meaning for you? Why?

The greatest good you can do for another is not just to share
your riches, but to reveal to him his own.
—Benjamin Disraeli

Few things help an individual more than to place responsi-
bility upon him and to let him know that you trust him.
—Booker T. Washington

Jesus came to them and said, "All authority in heaven and
on earth has been given to me. Therefore go and make
disciples of all nations, baptizing them in the name of the
Father and of the Son and of the Holy Spirit, and teaching
them to obey everything I have commanded you. And surely
I am with you always, to the very end of the age."
—Matthew 28:18–20

Passing the Baton

Michael Phelps had already won five gold medals in the 2004 Athens Olympics, and he seemed certain to secure one more in the 4 x 400 medley relay. But Michael's teammate, Ian Crocker, had not been so fortunate. Fighting flu symptoms all week, Ian's performance had been well below par. Just as it appeared that Ian would go home without a medal, Michael Phelps gave up his position in the 4 x 400 medley relay, giving his teammate a shot at the gold.

When he was told of the gesture, Ian Crocker nearly wept. "I'm kind of speechless," he said. "It's a huge gift that's difficult to accept. It makes me want to go out and tear up the pool."[1]

"It makes me want to go out and tear up the pool." Michael Phelps gave his teammate a priceless gift, one that is so often missing in our cut-throat society these days: the gift of empowerment. With motivation stirred to life because of his teammate's gift, Ian Crocker went on to help his team shatter its own record and take home the gold.

The second mile is not only the place in which we learn how to emerge victorious in our own race; it is also the place from which we are called by God to empower others to run.

This is exactly what Paul was doing when he wrote his letter to Philemon, a dear friend and fellow worker.

Paul was "passing the baton" to Philemon—he was giving him an opportunity to win. This letter is known as one of the Prison Epistles, because Paul was imprisoned in Rome when he wrote it.

Philemon was a slave owner, but he was also a man who loved God and who had a church in his home. Philemon had a slave, Onesimus, who had stolen from him, but who later became a Christian and was subsequently mentored by Paul.

As Paul prepared to send Onesimus back to Philemon, he issued a challenge to Philemon that was intended to empower him to run his own second mile:

I always thank my God as I remember you in my prayers, because I hear about your faith in the Lord Jesus and your love for all saints. I pray that you may be active in sharing your faith, so that you will have a full understanding of every good thing we have in Christ. Your love has given me great joy and encouragement, because you, brother, have refreshed the hearts of the saints.

Therefore, although in Christ I could be bold and order you to do what you ought to do, yet I appeal to you on the basis of love. I then, as Paul—an old man and now also a prisoner of Christ Jesus—I appeal to you for my son Onesimus, who became my son while I was in chains. Formerly he was useless to you, but now he has become useful both to you and to me.

I am sending him—who is my very heart— back to you. I would have liked to keep him with me so that he could take your place in helping me while I am in chains for the gospel. But I did not want to do anything without your consent, so that any favor you do will be spontaneous and not forced. Perhaps the reason he was separated from you for a little while was that you might have him back for good—no longer as a slave, but better than a slave, as a dear brother. He is very dear to me but even dearer to you, both as a man and as a fellow believer in the Lord.

So if you consider me a partner, welcome him as you would welcome me. If he has done you any wrong or owes you anything, charge it to me. I, Paul, am writing this with my own hand. I will pay it back—not to mention that you owe me your very self. I do wish, brother, that I may have some benefit from you in the Lord; refresh my heart in Christ. Confident of your obedience, I write to you, knowing that you will do even more than I ask.

—Philemon 4-21

Paul was making it clear to Philemon that life is a race, and in order to run it successfully, we must detach ourselves from everything that gets in our way. The Bible puts it this way: *Therefore, since we are surrounded by such a great cloud of witnesses, let us throw off everything that hinders and the sin that so easily entangles, and let us run with perseverance the race marked out for us* (Hebrews 12:1).

This was the kind of race that Paul was empowering Philemon to run when he wrote to him from prison. Paul wanted Philemon to know that if he did not run his race with fervor and passion, if he did not run it with perseverance and conviction, there would be no one available to carry the baton when he was finished.

In essence, Paul was saying to Philemon, "I want you to understand that God has brought to me a man who was your slave, who stole from you, but he has since encountered and accepted Christ. So now, Philemon, we have got to use this man, because he has become part of our relay team."

Paul wanted Philemon to view Onesimus not as a slave, but as the person he could become in Christ. Paul knew that if he empowered Philemon to run, in turn, Philemon could then empower Onesimus to run.

God has not only called us to go a second mile, but He has also enabled us to empower others to do the same thing. But if we, like Paul, are to issue successful challenges to others, we must also back them up and empower them to be victorious, especially at the beginning of their race, or they might not be able to finish. Paul knew this, which is why he issued his challenge to Philemon based on love.

There are three specific things that Paul did in this love-based letter that empowered Philemon to run his second mile:

- First, Paul affirmed Philemon by showing his appreciation for his friend.

- Second, he appealed to Philemon based on who he was in Christ.
- And third, Paul gave his assurance of payment.

Through Jesus Christ, God has given you everything you need in order to run the race He has marked for you—and to finish in victory. But you have the ability to empower others to run, as well. As you begin to affirm others, to appeal to them based on who they are in Christ, and to assure them of God's payment and rewards, you will experience a new level of God's provision and blessing in your own life. So get ready to pass the baton and move toward victory!

Affirmation and Appreciation

When U.S. gymnast Carly Patterson won the silver medal at the world championships in 2003, Mary Lou Retton, the only American woman to ever win all-around gymnastics gold, took notice and sent Carly a poster to encourage her. On the poster, Mary Lou wrote the words "I saw you win silver at the worlds, but I'll see gold on you in Athens!"

Carly Patterson hung that poster on her bedroom

wall, using the note of encouragement from Mary Lou Retton to fuel her passionate preparation for the Athens games. And after winning the gold medal in the all-around competition, who was the first person she called to share her good news? Mary Lou.[2]

The people around you need to hear your appreciation of what they've already done—and your affirmation of what you know they can do in the future. Paul expressed these sentiments in his letter to Philemon: *I always thank my God as I remember you in my prayers, because I hear about your faith in the Lord Jesus and your love for all the saints* (verse 4).

Paul wrote these words for a reason: He was about to ask Philemon to do something that would require more of him than had ever been required before. Paul used what I call a "spiritual stretch" or a "spiritual warm-up"; he communicated to Philemon that he was thankful for his work and affirmed his faith and love for the believers. And then Paul wrote, *I pray that you may be active in sharing your faith, so that you will have a full understanding of every good thing we have in Christ* (verse 6). Paul wanted Philemon to be reminded of what he had been given in Christ; he wanted him to understand that the situation with Onesimus was not as important as who Philemon was in Christ and who Christ was in him.

Paul then went on to write: *Your love has given me great joy and encouragement, because you, brother, have refreshed the hearts of the saints* (verse 7). Paul shared his heart, letting Philemon know what an encouragement his love had been since Philemon had chosen to be a part of Paul's life—and his race that had entered the second mile.

There was a reason that Paul took the time to affirm Philemon before he did anything else. Paul held a position of authority over Philemon and could have required him to alter his behavior toward Onesimus. But Paul chose instead to make a love-based appeal to Philemon's heart. He knew that if Philemon had a change of heart, it would change his life.

Today, there are tens of thousands of men and women who are ex-alcoholics and ex-drug addicts in this country—but they are not that way because they made a choice to quit. They were found guilty in a court of law and incarcerated, resulting in "forced reha-bilitation" because their drugs and alcohol were taken away. Some people might say, "But now they are drug and alcohol free!" Not really. The system is preventing them from getting drunk or high—they're not behaving that way because of any remorse or attitude adjustment. *They had a geographical change, not a change of heart.*

It is always God's desire that we pour into others the kind of heart-changing love that will lead them to love God, to serve Him, and to worship Him, based on their affirmation of His design and the deposit He made in their lives before they were born. What has to happen in the church, the business world, and the marketplace is that people must sense our heart for God as they observe the changes in our behavior. The reason believers *can* change is not because it is required, but because God's love gives us the will to follow Him.

As a father, I appreciate the way Paul came to Philemon with affirmation and appreciation. It would be easy to exercise authority over my children and say, "You will do exactly what I say in this home because I am in charge!"

Or I can look at my children and say, "You know what? When you were in your mother's womb, God was building greatness in you. He has a purpose for your life and a divine destiny for you. I want you to live out that destiny. I want you to know that greater is God in your life than the devil in this world. I want you to know that you were designed for greatness!"

By talking to them this way, by appreciating and affirming them I am putting something into their hearts that will cause them to believe in purpose and destiny. They will know that they were created and designed before they even drew a breath. When I speak to them this way, I am not altering their behavior—I am altering their hearts. And out of their hearts they can begin to live their lives based on love. Paul knew this, which is why he made his appeal to Philemon based on love.

I recently read a wonderful story about how the CEO of one of the world's major computer manufacturing corporations went about recruiting the thirty-eight-year-old president of a global soft-drink company. He did it by issuing this tremendous challenge to the younger man: "Do you want to spend the rest of your life selling sugared water or do you want to change the world?"

The CEO understood that if he simply offered the

young man more money, more benefits, or more vacation time, all he would get was his mind. But if he could convince this candidate that by joining the company he could change the world, he would have his heart. The vision would be woven into the fabric of his heart.

Right now, you have the ability to sow vision into the hearts and lives of others. Regardless of what stage of development you are in as a believer, there is always someone who can benefit from your experience and your affirmation. Find someone else whom you can help to get ready to run their second mile. Affirm them and let them know how much they are appreciated. Tell them that the second mile is the place where they will learn to overcome life's obstacles and emerge victorious. And as you pass the baton to these new second-mile runners, let them know they have the potential to change the world!

Appeals

The New England Patriots were a surprising success in the first half of the 2003-2004 NFL season. Despite using eight rookies to replace injured veterans, the Patriots led the AFC Eastern division with a 7-2 record.

Part of their success was due to an unselfish mindset adopted by players and coaches alike. The vice president of player personnel, Scott Pioli, displays a sign in his office that summarizes his attitude. The sign reads: "WE ARE BUILDING A TEAM—NOT COLLECTING TALENT."[3]

The team went on to win Super Bowl XXXVIII and their string of consecutive victories continued into the 2004-2005 season. Before finally losing on October 31, 2004, the team had established an NFL record of twenty-one straight wins—all by putting team above talent. Scott Pioli's sign was the *appeal* to both coaches and players to maintain their focus on the right thing—and by so doing, to reach success.

At a point in Paul's letter to Philemon, he shifted from affirmation to an appeal. Paul understood that before he could make an appeal to Philemon that would be effective, he first had to encourage and affirm what Philemon had already done. After that, he began his appeal: *Therefore, although in Christ I could be bold and order you to do what you ought to do, yet I appeal to you on the basis of love* (verse 8). Paul was saying: "I have deposited truth into your life. And now I am coming to you with an appeal based on love that will really test your love for Christ."

Paul continued: *I appeal to you for my son Onesimus, who became my son while I was in chains. Formerly he was useless to you, but now he has become useful both to you and to me* (verses 10–11). At this point, Paul began to put a spin on the name *Onesimus*, which means "profitable." Before he had come to Christ, the name given to Onesimus was not working, just as prior to all of our conversions to Christ, who we are does not work. But because the once useless slave had an encounter with Jesus Christ, he became "profitable" to both Paul and Philemon.

Paul's appeal was not only for the disobedient slave, but it was for himself, as well, because Onesimus had become his "son in the faith." In essence, what Paul was saying to Philemon was, "Onesimus is family to me now. I'm asking you to pull on your Christian love and understand that God has done a supernatural thing in this man named Onesimus. He has proved himself to be a genuine saint, a lover of God and a brother in Christ. I am basing my appeal to you on love."

So often, Christians try to wield their authority in

Christ in order to accomplish the things that they feel God wants them to do. What Paul does in this letter to motivate Philemon will work better than any practical information we could ever find in even the best management book available.

When authority is abused, people will often attempt to make an extreme, out-of-balance swing to a place where there is no authority. But Paul's words give us a perfect example of balance. Paul knew he had rights, but he chose not to exercise those rights. Instead, he appealed to Philemon to do the right thing. Paul wanted Philemon to do what he was asking based on love, not because of Paul's authority over him. Paul was trying to pull the "want to" out of Philemon.

I like to tell people, "You were created with a gift and a talent from God, and you are called to make a difference." I want to affirm the fact that each person is created in the image and likeness of God, and He has deposited great resources within them. God has equipped each one of us with exactly what we need to run the second mile, and He has enabled us to empower others to do the same. It is so important for each of us to run the second mile because if we don't, there will be a "gospel generation gap," a time in which the gospel of Jesus Christ is not proclaimed on this earth.

So Paul understood the importance of what he was saying to Philemon: "I am an old man, bound by chains and sitting in prison. And Philemon, you're not exactly a young pup, either . . . but you know what? You have got to pass the baton. You have got to put something into Onesimus that will cause him to know you believe in him. You need to empower him to run the second mile."

Paul was appealing to Philemon to not only run his own second mile, but also to empower Onesimus to do the same. Paul wanted Philemon to encourage Onesimus to run the kind of race that is expressed in the letter to the Hebrews:

Therefore, since we are surrounded by such a great cloud of witnesses, let us throw off everything that hinders and the sin that so easily entangles, and let us run with perseverance the race marked out for us. Let us fix our eyes on Jesus, the author and perfecter of our faith, who for the joy set before him endured the cross, scorning its shame, and sat down at the right hand of the throne of God. Consider him who endured such opposition from sinful men, so that you will not grow weary and lose heart.

—Hebrews 12:1–3

There are people in heaven that are cheering us on when they see us empower others to run! I can just see Isaiah standing up and, as he starts to wave, Jeremiah rises, too. Then Deborah gets up and begins to cheer: "Go team, go! Pass the baton of hope!" All the men and women who have laid down their lives for the gospel begin to shout from the coliseums of glory: "Don't drop the baton!"

What Paul was saying to Philemon was this: "Philemon, don't drop the baton. My appeal is based on the love of God and the power of Jesus Christ. The coliseums of heaven are waiting with anticipation to see what you are going to do about this slave. It's your decision."

Right now, open your spiritual eyes to see the great cloud of witnesses that is pulling for you to run with perseverance the race that is marked for you. Today, you hold in your hand one of many batons that God has given you to pass along to others. And the way to pull them alongside of you in order to receive that baton is to appeal to them based on the love of Christ. Each time you appeal to another believer who receives the baton of hope, shouts of glory will ring throughout the coliseums of heaven as you and your team press on to victory!

Assurance of Payment

After Paul made his appeal to Philemon, he sealed it with his assurance of payment: *So if you consider me a partner, welcome him as you would welcome me. If he has done you any wrong or owes you anything, charge it to me. I, Paul, am writing this with my own hand. I will pay it back* (verses 17–19).

Now Paul's statement here doesn't mean that every time we make an appeal to another believer to do what is right that we should be willing to literally assume the financial responsibility. But there is a principle that is being given that we need to understand.

Paul had already told Philemon that Onesimus had become his "son," indicating that Paul had led him to

Jesus. Therefore, Paul was his father in the faith. At the point in time we come to Jesus Christ and are born again, God becomes our heavenly Father. So when Paul said "charge it to me," he was emulating our heavenly Father's desire to meet our every need.

I once had an experience that demonstrated this powerful principle. A few years ago, my youngest child learned that in the corner of the bookstore at Victory Church is a refreshment center, complete with a beverage bar and a candy rack. And by the time she had turned three, she had learned that the best way to move that little bag of M&M's from the candy shelf and into her pocket was to take it to the cashier and say, "Charge it to my daddy!"

God wants us to have that same kind of confidence in Him when we step out to empower others to run their second mile. I am constantly amazed at the testimonies about God's provision that come from people who serve at our church. Although they are different ages and have different backgrounds, there is one thing they have in common: They each have a desire to serve God by using the gifts and talents He has given them in order to empower other people.

One dear woman in her early 80s has the most beautiful smile that touches everyone with whom she comes in contact. She never misses a service or the opportunity to tell people about God's goodness. When her husband died a few years ago, she discovered that the stock in which they had invested was worthless. She had become a widow with an uncertain future. But this second-mile grandma knew that she could count on her heavenly Father's care, and it wasn't long before the windows of heaven opened up and began to pour out blessings upon her. She received several cash settlements, a substantial increase in her Social Security income, an unexpected inheritance, and numerous other gifts and surprises. And she continues to be an amazing source of encouragement as she passes batons on to other second-mile runners.

One young couple, I'll call them Bill and Sue, has served faithfully at Victory Church since they began attending. She is part of the children's ministry, and he is an usher. Although it took their combined incomes to meet the needs of their family of five, Sue felt that God wanted her to be at home during this stage of her children's lives. After seeking God through prayer about His timing, she and Bill agreed it was time to trust God to meet their needs with Bill's paycheck alone. Soon after Sue quit her job, Bill received the professional certification he needed to enable him to command a much higher salary. These second-mile teammates continue to run their own race while empowering others to do the same.

And then there is the story of the woman who had been the manager of a national retail store for seventeen years. During that time, she had been involved at Victory Church for a number of years in several different capacities, but she had a real gift of working with incarcerated women and men. She wanted to spend 100 percent of her time empowering them to be all they could be in Jesus Christ, but she didn't know how to do it and still pay her bills. So she began to seek God about her situation. Then one day she heard her heavenly Father say, *Trust Me,* and she knew that it was time for her to step out. Today she is passing the baton to hundreds of men and women in prisons throughout our state, empowering them to run their races successfully despite their circumstances. Because she was in God's will and in His timing, she knew that as far as her needs were concerned, she could "charge it to Daddy"—and all of her needs have been taken care of.

Although each one of these people has come to the place where they are empowering others to run, there was a time when someone did the same for them. And with the appeal that pulled something great out of each of them came the assurance of God's payment.

We all know that anything worth having is going to cost us something. Paul understood that, and He was willing to pay the price in order to give Onesimus the opportunity to run his race. The price we must pay is our willingness to invest our lives in service to others, empowering them to run their own second mile.

Right now, you have within you everything you need in order to do just that. Although you have the authority of God's Word from which you can issue a second-mile challenge, you already know that the best way to issue a challenge is on the basis of love.

You have the ability to appeal to others based on the gifts and talents that God has placed within them. Your appeal to them to serve God by serving others lays the groundwork for them to receive the baton and then pass it on again.

Don't be concerned about the cost because God has already paid the price for each of us to run our own race. Because of the price He paid, we can confidently tell others to "charge it to Daddy" as we pass the baton and empower them to run the race that God has laid out for their lives.

M I L E   M A R K E R S

➤ Think of someone in your life who needs affirmation or encouragement. What can you do to help motivate them as they run their second mile?

➤ Have you ever been motivated to do something out of fear, or because you were forced to do it? Have you ever been motivated through love? What difference did it make in your attitude—and in the results?

➤ What costs are you facing today that you need to "charge to Daddy"? Offer your needs to Him in prayer, asking Him for His provision, not only so that you would be blessed, but so that you would be a blessing and an encouragement to others.

It is the end that crowns us, not the fight.
—Robert Herrick

Bad will be the day for every man when he becomes absolutely contented with the life he is living, when there is not forever beating at the doors of his soul some great desire to do something larger.
—Phillips Brooks

Thanks be to God who gives us the victory through our Lord Jesus Christ!
—1 Corinthians 15:57 TEV

Crossing the Finish Line

9

Pat Tillman loved football. But he loved his freedom as an American more.

When Pat arrived at Arizona State as a freshman in 1994, he managed to land the school's last remaining football scholarship. At first that translated into a spot on the end of the bench, but by the time Pat graduated summa cum laude from Arizona State, he was no bench-sitter. Pat Tillman was named the Pac-10's Conference Defensive Player of the Year—and he was chosen by the Arizona Cardinals in the 1998 NFL draft.

Pat refused to be put off by the fact that he was the 226th pick out of 241 to be drafted. Five months later, despite his undersized 5'11', 200-pound frame, he had become Arizona's starting strong safety. And several seasons later, in 2001, he was offered a $9 million five-year contract by the St. Louis Rams. Pat declined the offer out of loyalty to the team that had drafted him—that's the kind of person that he was.

After the terrorist attacks of September 11, 2001, the twenty-five-year old superstar began to reevaluate his priorities. And in the spring of 2002, just after returning from his honeymoon, Pat announced his decision to leave the team after only four seasons—even though it meant turning down a three-year, $3.6 million contract. Instead, Tillman felt called to lay aside his privileged life in order to defend the country that had allowed him to succeed. In May 2002, Pat enlisted in the U.S. Army as a Ranger, and following basic training, he was deployed in the Persian Gulf. He went from the status of a millionaire to having an annual salary of just $18,000.

On Thursday, April 22, 2004, Pat Tillman was killed in Afghanistan during a firefight with anti-coalition militia forces. Former Cardinals head coach Dave McGinnis had this to say about Pat's sacrifice: "Pat Tillman represented all that was good in sports. He knew his purpose in life and proudly walked away from a career in football to a greater calling."[1]

Pat Tillman was a success by the world's standards—but he knew there were greater victories to achieve. He chose to travel the second mile, to give his life for others rather than focusing on the successes he had already achieved. In order for us to emerge victorious in every situation we face in life, we must do the same: develop a "second-mile mentality," and see to it that it becomes part of the fabric of our being.

Jesus knew this as He spoke to His disciples on the mountainside: *"If someone forces you to go one mile, go with him two miles"* (Matthew 5:41). He knew that in order for them to successfully complete the race that God had given each one of them to run, they had to be willing to do much more than just what was required of them. The same is true for us.

We each have a lifelong race to run. It is filled with

both obstacles and opportunities for accomplishment every step of the way. The good news is that God has already marked out our track by His Word. And in His Word we can find everything we need to overcome each obstacle and take advantage of every opportunity that is presented to us.

There are those who will choose to view the second mile as nothing more than a difficult place from which they hope to be removed—as quickly as possible—so that they can return to their comfort zones and go on living life in the same way they always have. But there are others who, like Pat Tillman, will embrace the inevitable challenges of the second mile. The second mile is the place where we receive the blessings of God and emerge victorious—and where we begin to be a blessing to others.

We each have choices to make. We can choose to focus on the pains of our second mile, or we can set our sights on the gains that we make in the kingdom of God. We can race to win, or stop and whine. Remember, others are watching and will follow our attitudes and behavior.

Finishing the race does not mean that we are finished in life. As soon as we see victory in one battle, there will be another battle waiting for us to fight, right around the corner. As we grow in the Lord and follow the path He has laid out for us, we will build success upon success—until the race on this side is finished. On that day, the greatest and truest reward will come when we hear Him say those long-coveted words, *"Well done, My good and faithful servant!"*

But we will never hear those words if we don't finish the race! Quitters never win. If we don't persevere in this life, and run the second mile that God has laid out before us, we won't secure the victory in the battles of life. And we won't receive the victor's crown at the end of it all, when we finally reach heaven. I want to be counted among those who receive the "prize"—that great reward for which God has called me heavenward! I hope that you will run the race and be counted on that day with me.

My greatest prayer is that all of us begin to use every breath that we have to press on toward the mark of Christ:

Not that I have already obtained all this, or have already been made perfect, but I press on to take hold of that for which Christ Jesus took hold of me.

Brothers [and sisters], *I do not consider myself yet to have taken hold of it. But one thing I do: Forgetting what is behind and straining toward what is ahead, I press on toward the goal to win the prize for which God has called me heavenward in Christ Jesus.*

—Philippians 3:12–14

God has always had a purpose for each and every generation. The Bible says, *For when David had served God's purpose in his own generation, he fell asleep; he was buried with his fathers* (Acts 13:36). The baton that represents the responsibility for the good news of the gospel is now in the hands of our generation. Let's not drop it, because heaven and earth are depending on us. Let's run!

MILE MARKERS

- What "finish lines" have you crossed victoriously in your life so far?
- What "finish lines" do you see just ahead?
- In what areas do you need to choose to run the race God wants you to run? How have you run this race so far? How can you press on to run the second mile?
- What can you do in your life, right now, that will someday bring the words of affirmation, *"Well done, My good and faithful servant!"*?

I am not afraid of tomorrow,
for I have seen yesterday and
I love today.
—William Allen White

Not that I have already
obtained all this, or have
already been made perfect,
but I press on to take hold of
that for which Christ Jesus
took hold of me.
—Philippians 3:12

Notes

Foreword

[1]Julia H. Johnston, *Fifty Missionary Heroes* (New York: Fleming Revell, 1913).

Chapter 1: On Your Mark, Get Set, Go!

[1]"Rower Suffers Aussie Backlash," *www.News.BBC.Co.uk*, August 25, 2004.

Chapter 2: A Place of Miracles

[1]Adapted from "Olympian Steven Bradbury: The Last Became First," *www.reuters.com*, February 17, 2002.

[2]Chuck Swindoll, quoted in Bob Reccord, *Forged by Fire: How God Shapes Those He Loves* (Nashville: Broadman & Holman, 2000), 118.

[3]Adapted from Barbara Royce, "Maria and the Halo," *Christian Reader*, July/August 2001, 63.

[4]Guido Kuwas, *Global Revival News*, December 17, 2001.

Chapter 3: Setting an Example for Others

[1]Boyd Clarke and Ron Crossland, *The Leader's Voice* (Select Books, 2002).

[2]Grace Fox, "What Makes DeeDee Run?" *Christian Reader* (Nov./Dec. 2002), 28–29.

[3]Greg Miller, quoted at *www.clarionledger.com*, accessed April 18, 2004.

[4]Gary Thomas, *Sacred Marriage* (Grand Rapids: Zondervan, 2000), 36–37.

[5]Ibid.

[6]Richard Carol Hoefler, *And He Told Them a Story* (C.S.S. Publishing, 1979).

[7]Bob Carlisle, *Sons: A Father's Love* (Nashville: W Publishing, 1999).

[8]Leith Anderson, *Leadership That Works* (Minneapolis: Bethany House, 1999), 164–165.

[9]Marsha Marks, "Special Delivery," *Christian Reader* (Sep./Oct. 2000), 15–17.

Chapter 4: The Place of Second Chances

[1]John Ortberg, *If You Want to Walk on Water, You Have to Get Out of the Boat* (Grand Rapids: Zondervan, 2001).

[2]John Wiley and Sons Publishing Company, *The Book of Leadership Wisdom: Classic Writings by Legendary Business Leaders* (John Wiley and Sons, 1998), 326.

[3]David Mordkoff, "American Emmons Misses Out on Gold by Firing at Wrong Target," *www.sports.yahoo.com*, accessed on August 22, 2004.

[4]Christin Ditchfield, *Power Up.*

[5]Jim Wilson, *Future Church*, (Serendipity House, 2002), 155.

[6]*Hoosiers*, written by Angelo Pizzo, directed by David Anspaugh, produced by Hemdale Film Corporation, 1986.

[7]Dr. James Dobson, "Focus on the Family" broadcast, January 2005.

Chapter 5: Jumping the Hurdles

[1]Brennan Manning in the foreword to James Bryan Smith, *Rich Mullins: His Life and Legacy* (Broadman & Holman, 2000), xi.

[2]dcTalk, *Jesus Freaks* (Tulsa: Albury, 1999).

[3]Ibid.

Chapter 6: Getting Your Second Wind

[1]Greg Asimakoupoulis, *New York Times*, September 20, 2000.

[2]Paul Lambourne Higgins, "Selections from the Journal of John Wesley," *Upper Room Magazine*, 1967, 30–31.

Chapter 7: Learning from Jesus

[1]Laura Lee, "The Worst Predictions of All Time," *The Futurist* (September/October 2000), 20–25.

[2]Jia-Rui Chong, "Disney Hall Glare Gets to Neighbors," *The Los Angeles Times*, February 21, 2004.

[3]Ken Landis, Rex Gunn, and Robert Andrade, *Deceit at Pearl Harbor.*

Chapter 8: Passing the Baton

[1]Mike Teirney, "Phelps Cedes Spotlight to Struggling Teammate," *Atlanta Journal Constitution*, August 21, 2004.

[2]E. M. Swift, cited in *Sports Illustrated*, August 30, 2004, 49.

[3]Peter King, "Center of Attention," *Sports Illustrated*, November 3, 2004, 94.

Chapter 9: Crossing the Finish Line

[1]Compiled from *AOL News*, April 23, 2004, and *NFL Insider*, March 20, 2003.

About the Author

M ark Crow, along with his wife, Jennifer, pastor Victory Church, in Oklahoma City, which they founded in 1994. Mark's ministry philosophy was not to build a church, but to build people to live life victoriously in Jesus. With over 8,000 members, 12,000 decisions for Christ, and planting churches in other cities across America, Mark's motto, "You were born for victory," is reflected not on a church wall, but on the hearts and in the lives of men and women.

For information on the weekly TV show, **The Art of Living**, or information about Mark Crow and Victory Church, visit the church's Web site at *www.victorychurch.tv*.

Victory Church is located at 4300 North MacArthur, Oklahoma City, OK 73122.

VICTORY
CHURCH.TV

The Art of Living weekly TV program is broadcast on the Daystar Network in over 130 countries. Visit our website at www.victorychurch.tv for local times and listings.

The following are available wherever fine books are sold.